# A S…
# CALLED
# Bambi

## SHED SOCIETAL EXPECTATIONS

### A THERAPIST'S GUIDE TO AUTHENTIC LIVING AND INNER PEACE

ASHLEIGH DUNCAN MBACP
PSYCHOTHERAPEUTIC COUNSELLOR

This edition first published in paperback by
Michael Terence Publishing in 2024
www.mtp.agency



ISBN 9781800948112



Cover design (AI)
Michael Terence Publishing
www.mtp.agency

# Contents

# Introduction

*A Stripper Called Bambi.* You might have reached for this book in the hope of reading some antidotes about the life of a stripper called Bambi, if that is your expectation, it is best to set the book down now as the content of this book could not be further from a day in the life of a stripper. However, this book certainly aims to disrobe, but rather than stripping off our clothes, it contains tales, lessons and analogies to strip down the ego, disrobe from the expectations of society, undressing from the pressures of life and letting go of most of the things we have learnt to date, all with a view of reframing, rebuilding and redressing in a way that suits our own unique style, our individual philosophical needs and personal values.

Let's get straight to the point. Suffering is an inevitable part of the human experience, an invisible thread woven into the story of our lives. As humans we are averse to suffering, we try exceptionally hard not to suffer, trying to control, protect, deflect and think and avoid our way out of suffering, however, suffering is a big part of the human experience whether we like it or not. Think of suffering to be like the weather, we have many adverse weather conditions, some unpleasant and often an inconvenience to our plans. Can we control it? No, nor do we try to. We just accept it and do what we can to make it more bearable until it passes. The human experience and emotions are similar. We explore this in detail in the passage **"Life Is Tough – it's said that no one comes out alive"**.

For example, rain is an inevitable unavoidable weather condition. So, what do we do when it rains? Well, we have two choices really.

**Choice 1**
**Avoid it. Don't leave the house, skip that walk or cancel our day out. Stay within our comfort zone, basically miss out.**

**Choice 2**
**We put on a raincoat, waterproof clothing or use a brolly. We equip ourselves for such conditions with the aim of protecting ourselves and make the most of the conditions we find ourselves in.**

At times this can relate to the challenges of life; you see, every adverse or painful situation causes us to pick one of these options, we either live a life trying to avoid the hurt or suffering and/or we layer up in self- protection which in my opinion causes its own hurt or suffering. In our quest to protect ourselves we can develop a self-protective narrative; this can range from several emotional and behavioural issues which may lead to self-protective believes that are limiting.

**Below are some common examples of the behaviour that breeds these beliefs.**

| Behaviour | Self-protective Belief |
|---|---|
| Staying in our comfort zone | We are comfortable and safe here. |
| Anxiety | If we are hyperaware, we can prepare for it. |
| Negative thoughts | If we expect the worst, we can deal with it better. |
| Attachment issues | If we don't get close, we can't be hurt or let down. |
| Self-worth issues | I deserve this treatment. |

Developing these unhealthy coping mechanisms is an unconscious form of self-protection, because if we protect ourselves from these things, we can't get hurt. Right?

Wrong.

We simply suffer longer and unnecessarily so or suffer twice. How many times have you worried over a non-occurrence? Something you thought that would happen but never did. What an absolute waste of our precious time and energy. We may have also done some interpersonal damage along the way. Take a moment to consider how worrying serves you? Reflect on how it might feel to really let go of worry, lean into the now and fully accept the situations that come your way with a view of responding to them rather than reacting. How might it feel to be calm and regulated in the day to day.

This book aims to help us live more presently, accept suffering as part of the human experience and live a fulfilling life of contentment and peace. It contains 21 short stories, memorable phrases and lessons to soothe in times of discomfort. It outlines simple teachings and techniques to navigate the challenges of life. The teachings within aspire to curate a different outlook, reframe our limiting beliefs and see the world from an outlook of presence and patience curating for full acceptance for the here and now. To make such changes we need to address, undress and redress. Now, please don't take this literally, I know the book title refers to a stripper, but I am not asking anyone to undress their clothing, what I am suggesting is we undress the protective layers life has adorned us in, that we step out of self-pseudo and reconnect with our authentic self, the self that was pure and free before life dressed us.

I know this may sound scary, undressing leaves us naked, being naked makes us feel exposed and vulnerable but that is the journey of self-awareness and only through self-awareness, presence and grace can healing occur. When we undress remember that we have full autonomy to redress however we like! To explore, experiment and express how we are feeling on that day or parts of our personality we wish to share. We wash the clothes of yesterday and start fresh each day. Imagine life was like that! I'm here to tell you it can be. Each day we can start a fresh. Learn from yesterday and move forward. Therapeutically undressing and redressing is simply self-expression, self-awareness and accepting our self-worth.

Now, the analogy of undressing from a therapeutic perspective is not the only reason I named a personal development book "A Stripper Called Bambi" the similitude of undressing not only worked well for the intention of the book, it is in fact that an actual stripper called Bambi has somewhat inspired the name of this book, not only the name of the book but I believe had a major influence on how my life has progressed which in turn has influenced me to share my thoughts on paper. I do not know Bambi, my relationship with Bambi was very fleeting I recall only one simple exchange with Bambi, that exchange had such an impact on me, a perfect demonstration of the influence we can have on others. The impact we have on others is bigger than we can ever really know, I am sure Bambi has absolutely no idea that her kindness held such weight. That for me has been another life lesson as doing the work that I do, I often see the depth of suffering or self-belief that humanity can have on one another, I hold this in my conscious intention giving careful consideration to my words and behaviours towards others, aspiring to lead with compassion, with that being said we are human, each with our own vulnerabilities and beautiful flaws, therefore we aren't perfect, but do have the power to heal and cause the suffering of another, and through our own wants, ego and protection we will do both, no questions, we will be both the cause and the cure for hurt. Explored further in the passage **"The Art of Empathy – the gift of healing"**.

In 2005 at the tender age of 18 I left my hometown in Northern Ireland with a few good friends to do a season in Ibiza. I'd always somewhat struggled with a curious mind, and itchy feet, feeling quite suppressed at life in a small country, from a young age I felt a bit different to my peers, I craved spirituality, freedom and adventure, something that was lacking in my environment at that time. Just recently I came across a framed picture I'd framed in primary school, behind the frame I had hid a list of intentions, one being to live in a different country with a beach, I dated this in 1996 making me around 10 when I wrote it, bear in mind this was way before manifesting was a thing!! Magically the things I had written and forgotten about at the young age of 10 have all came to fruition. I had also written I wanted a job helping people, I have been a professional counsellor for 10 years, I work in private practice and have successfully worked with 1,000s of clients throughout my time as a therapist, to each one I am very grateful to share the therapeutic journey with, being a therapist is such a privilege. Up until my late 20s I had no idea this is where my life would take me, I started my career in PR and then moved into the cooperate world never really settling or feeling satisfied. I became a counsellor by pure chance, this career change presented itself during my own struggles, amid a change of circumstance I stumbled across a 12-week introduction to counselling course and signed up to it not really knowing what it was or having any intention of actually pursuing a career in therapy. A talk a little bit more about therapy in the passage **"A Soft Place to Land"**. The reason I chose the course was due to a separation, at that time my son was going to stay with his father every Tuesday evening, I couldn't bear the thought of not having my baby with me for a prolonged time each Tuesday so as a protective factor, (case in point) I went to my local college to sign up for any course that would distract me each Tuesday, I didn't care what the course was, looking back I think the college receptionist thought I was a bit nuts, I went down and asked to be enrolled on a course on a Tuesday evening.

"What course are you interested in?"

"One on a Tuesday please"

"But which one?"

"Just one on a Tuesday, I'm interested in a course on Tuesday."

"OKayyy." Looking slightly sceptical or scared. "Do you have any specific interests?'

"Tuesdays please."

I'm surprised she enrolled me on anything to be honest. Fair play. It just so happens it was a counselling course, I thank my lucky stars for this diversion in my path regularly as I absolutely love what I do. After the 12 weeks introduction I decided to progress, the next level wasn't even on a Tuesday! I continued my studies and placement, again, with no expectations or intention, I found the work fascinating, and luckily had a natural ability to form a compassionate connection with those I worked with, thanks to an incredible tutor, supportive classmates, the kindness of other counsellors and of course the guidance from my wonderful supervisor I pursued a successful career in counselling opening up my own private practice straight after graduation.

On a lighter note, in my young manifesting intention setting, I also wrote I wanted a white dog; my brother surprised me with a white dog on my 24th birthday (earth angel – I'm talking about the dog btw). Anyway, I have digressed, I do that, but most creative thinkers do, people see it as a weakness but trust me it's a strength. Understood, accepted and used correctly every character attribute is a strength, we just need to appreciate the diversity and potential within.

I've never been a conventional person, I'm pretty defiant and tend to rebel against the conformations of society, I am a deep thinker, with a curious mind. Being a free thinker can cause a struggle with societal expectations, when it came to leaving school, I couldn't think of anything worse than living in the box that society expected of us.

I struggled in the school system, as many people I speak with do. To me, it felt suffocating and rigid, it seemed that we were all expected to be and perform the same, yet we were all so very different. Many people can feel different while to the school system, the environment can elicit various emotions and experiences amongst individuals. The system promotes conformity and standardised learning, which may not fit to the unique strengths, learning style and neurological needs of every student. This can make students feel like they don't fit in. Additionally, the emphasis on grades, competition and comparison in the school system can create a sense of pressure and self-doubt. Students who struggle academically or socially may somehow feel inadequate compared to their peers. These contributing factors can all lead to limiting core beliefs which can be detrimental to our self-esteem and confidence. This book aims to break these down with the view of reframing them, in the lesson **"What's Normal to the Spider is Chaos to the Fly"** we will go into more detail.

Young people are full of energy with a natural inclination to express their thoughts, however within the school system we are often instructed to suppress our thoughts, repress our natural urges, sit still and be quiet. When we break it down it sounds pretty tough! All whilst actively listening, processing the lesson, learning facts and paying attention, exhausting! Now I do understand this environment works for some, and many young people excel and thrive in the structure of the school system, but different people need different environments, the environment surrounding us can have a significant impact on our mental health and wellbeing we will deep dive this further in the passage

**"A Cactus Doesn't Live in the Dessert Because He Likes It".**

In black and white how obvious this seems. We as humans and individuals with different biology, physiology and backgrounds are all different, yet the school system expects us to be the same. Utter madness. In my humble opinion (by that I mean educated but I'm too humble to say) it's an old system in a new world, conditioning people to conform and suppressing the spirit of so many, how many people left the system thinking they were different or not enough? Too many. To which I am sure most therapists will agree with me, as many counsellors will tell you a vast amount of inner work is spent healing the wounds of this system, the limiting beliefs the system has created and even the core beliefs a comment from an educator has implanted, now, I do realise there are some fantastic education systems and teachers out there, helpers, healers, music makers and creators of light, those who are guiding students through their school years with compassion and empathy, those who are stepping outside the conventual teaching methods delivering a person centred teaching approach (praise be) and these guys are going to make such a difference in the young people of today, and those young people are going to be the change, as it is so I'm all about it!

So anyway, (told you, digressing) Ibiza was the perfect place to begin in my pursuit of happiness. The island itself has such a special energy and the people who flocked to the island each year all who were seeking their own individual quest of discovery. This beautiful bunch were the perfect blend of hedonism and epicureanism. Ibiza suited my personality, an island of partying and peace. Looking back now if there was one thing I would give myself and my peers at the time, was mindfulness, we were young and most definitely at the time took the whole experience for granted, sleeping in late and partying to the wee hours, if I was to do it all over again, I wouldn't do an absolute thing differently!! What I would give now to be walking up San Antonio's Westend on my way home from a superclub at 10am with dirty disco feet holding my besties hand and laughing our legs off at the antics of the night.

Living on an island like this had its ups and downs, as does life, we explore this further in the chapter **"Teardrops on the Dancefloor"**. Worker friends have referred to it as neverland, a magical place where we felt young, fun and carefree, but full of lost souls each seeking serendipity with an unmet need.

While staying in Ibiza, I still struggled to feel content, we discuss inner contentment in the passage **"Paving the Path"**. I overindulged, engaged in wreck less behaviour, sometimes getting myself into situations that on hindsight weren't that safe, but I guess that is part of growing up. I have never been and still am not averse to risk, coupled with a deep need for freedom and adventure on a party island with no rules a dangerous mix! I won't go into the nitty gritty details of this for now, but I used the island and all it offered as a form of escapism from whatever it was that I was trying to escape from as I believe that many people did and still do. While on the island I worked behind the bar in a strip club, I absolutely loved working there, we were well looked after by management and the energy was always high and the girls were such fun. While on shift one night after an extremely heavy night I was a bit down and contemplating the meaning of life (as you do). I remember feeling in a state of dissociation, genuinely contemplating flying home as the highs and lows were taking its toll on me though I had only been there a few weeks. In my state of misery, I was approached by a dancer I'd never met before; the dancers came and went so there wasn't much time to form relationships. Anyway, she introduced herself as "Bambi" saying she had always noticed my high energy and been attracted to it, but I didn't seem my usually bubbly self, and asked me was I ok. A compassionate act from Bambi. (We learn more about compassion in the later passage **"Compassion is the Cure"**.) She said she was only over for a few weeks as was a phycology student trying to get some money for her studies, and was leaving the island tomorrow, she handed me a book and told me she didn't need it anymore and to read it and made me promise I would start the book straight away. The book was "The Art of Happiness" by the Dali Lama. That simple exchange was the beginning of my relationship with self-discovery and Buddhism. For those who haven't read the book the book is written by the 14th Dalia Lama and Howard C Cutler, it is a book that explores the nature of true happiness, providing practical and spiritual teachings and advice on living mindfully and compassionately, the book taught me the importance of presence and living in the now. We explore this in the lesson **"Human Being or Human Doing"**.

For me this book was a gamechanger, I still have the exact book and still 20 years on visit it occasionally. Reading the book inspired a deeper need to learn more about a different way to live, inspired me to connect with myself on a mindful, spiritual and compassionate level, 3 ingredients which I believe are the antidote to a content life. I took the advice and teachings and curated my life around them; I have since read 100s of similar books, attended Buddhist and spiritual teachings and retreats, self-development talks and workshops and of course developed my own professional education and career. Each lesson within this book comes from my own journey of self-discovery, educational, personal and professional experiences. Some you may relate to, some you may not, but just remember not all seeds planted grow straight away. I believe spiritually would have found me somewhere down my life path, but the book Bambi gave me came at a time when I needed it most and has served me through all my adult life. I hope this book comes at a time you need it most and the lessons within go onto serve you well.

# Life Is Tough

## – it's said that no one comes out alive

**A passage on living presently and contently, whilst accepting that the pain, and suffering of humanity is an essential aspect of the human experience that cannot be compromised.**

What a profound yet hard truth about the human experience, a fact of life is that life is inherently challenging and no matter who we are or what we do at several points throughout our life we will all face struggles, challenges, suffering and then eventually meet our mortality. This may sound like harsh actuality, but it is the reality of our human existence and as much as we may try, there is no escaping from reality. In fact, it is quite the opposite, the more we accept the reality of the human experience the easier this experience is, and the less precious time wasted spent trying to resist the inevitable.

### So how do we accept this grim reality I hear you ask?

Firstly, it's about living presently, this is achieved by fully accepting what is in the here and now, acknowledging the experience for what it is. Allowing the experience is the ability to permit and accept the somatic response the moment activates (a somatic response refers to a physical reaction that occurs in the body as a result of a stimulus or trigger. It can include various bodily sensations such as increased heart rate, anxiety, tension or changes in breathing, among other physical responses). Only when we fully embrace the sensations we experience and acknowledge the validity of our emotions, can we effectively regulate and manage them. Regulating the body involves remaining in a state of inner connection, a condition of balance and harmony, maintaining a sense of calm and mindfulness in the situation we are navigating. We can achieve regulation by tapping into various techniques as needed, such as touch points of the body, there are several touch points in the body that are known to help promote a sense of calm and relaxation, here are a few;

**Somatic Practices/Body Scan**

1. Chest – gently place your hand on your chest near your heart, can help you connect with the breath and bring a sense of calm and connection back into the body.
2. Forehead – Place your hand on your forehead and tenderly give it a gentle rub, this can help release tension.
3. Neck – Massage or apply light pressure to the back of neck, this will soothe any tension that is held there.
4. Hands – Rub your hands together briskly and place over your eyes can slow the mind.

Another example of a somatic technique is **body scanning.** In this practice you simply focus your attention on different parts of your body, starting from your toes to your head. As you scan each body pay intentional attention to the sensations or tension you may feel, consciously recognising or releasing any discomfort. This reaction helps to promote relaxation, body awareness and overall calm.

In acknowledging the moment for what it is we can embrace presence and engage wholeheartedly in the authentic experience. This involves being aware of our thoughts, emotions and physical sensations created by the moment, allowing ourselves to experience and process each. By regulating this response only then can we cultivate a greater sense of calmness, clarity and inner balance. Because what else really exists other than now? What is in the past is a memory and what is in the future is an illusion. The practice of living presently allows us to fully engage in our relationships, foster deeper connections, strengthen our sense of self and connect to ourselves on a spiritual level.

Once feeling calm and regulated it can be beneficial to identify what is within our control and what is not. Think about it, we spend so much time trying to control what we can't.

Ask yourself what really is within your control? If you journal this can be a valuable reflection. This is a question that comes up often in my therapeutic practice. I'm often recited the same answers. **Finances**, **relationships**, **career**, **social life**, and met with the same shock or fear when I gently disagree with the answer.

Many clients come to therapy presenting with a deep need to control whatever feeling or situation they find themselves battling, this need gets hungrier when a person is faced with situations or feelings that are outside their control, yet we do our darndest to deny the fact they can't control it. This can have a detrimental impact on a person's mental health and overall wellbeing and function. Realistically none of these are in your control. The only thing that is within your control is your reactions. Fear not, all is not lost, this are what we refer to in the therapy room as your circle of concern.

**Let's unpack it**

Finances/Career – sure, we can *manage* our finances, budget, save and invest, however our finances relay heavily on our employment or income source as well being dictated by our incomings/outgoings, inflation, the national cost of living amongst many other factors. We can all agree our employment or income source is out of our control, as this is subject to our employer/consumers. What we can do, is keep it in our concern i.e. manage, budget, save etc. Our career provides our finances, employment and pay grade may be out of our control but by choosing our career path, showing up to work each day and maintaining the expected work performance, we can keep this in our concern.

Relationships/social – in the realm of relationships we often find ourselves grasping for a strong level of control, for many people this need runs deep, this can vary from person to person and may be built on personal connections, attachment styles, and past relational experiences. According to Marslows Hierarchy of Needs a basic human need is safety, the need for safety is under-coupled with the need for security, trust, intimacy, acceptance, the ability to receive and give affection, as humans we yearn stability and predictably, however the actions of others are completely outside our control, we can keep these in our control by choosing who we spend time with, keeping boundaries in our relationships and communicating our expectations within our relationships.

**So what is in our control?**

What is in our control is our own actions, reactions, and behaviours. We can choose how we behave and interact with others. We have the power to choose what we react too and how we respond externally. We may not be able to control those around us, but we do have the autonomy to choose what treatment we accept from others and how we conduct our daily lives. We can choose compassion, kindness and understanding even in difficult situations. We can even choose how we respond to difficult people. By taking responsibility of our own actions and making conscious choices we can create a present and positive life regardless of what goes on around us.

Inner peace and contentment begin the moment you choose not to allow another person or external situation to control your actions, reactions or behaviours. If you can conquer regulating the internal, I promise the external will to feel more manageable.

To conclude, we cannot control or shield ourselves from the suffering of life, but with the right mindset, grace and presence we can certainly move though with gentle tenderness and compassion for ourselves during times of suffering.

Life will continuously test our resilience and character, but it is through overcoming these challenges that we grow and evolve as humans and individuals. Impermanence – no one comes out alive, highlights the inevitably of depth. This serves as a reminder that life is fragile and finite and that our time on this earth is limited. With this realisation let it inspire us to make the most of lives, cherish the moments that we have and truly prioritise what matters to us, because in my opinion all that really matters, is love and life itself, yet we spend our days worrying about what doesn't really matter, or trying to control what we cannot.

## Therapeutic Technique

A technique I often use in my personal life and offer to clients who attend therapy is the "Matter in 5" technique, if presented with a "micro drama or dilemma' I often ask, will this matter in 5 hours, 5 days, 5 weeks or 5 months. Often the answer is "no". The wonderful but challenging thing about our feelings is that they are fluid and fickle, they ebb and flow, and come and go. But rather than try to control them, simply allow them.

Lean into each emotion as it comes and let it go as it passes, because it will.

I once had a client say to me "I don't know if I'll ever stop crying". They had a genuine concern that the feeling they were experiencing would stay with them forever, because this is the thing, we get so stuck in our experiences in that moment that for while we carry the belief that moments last forever, but this is impossible.

I responded, "Do you know anyone who has never stopped crying?" The client cry laughed, you know that ugly snorty laughing cry when the body and brain become confused. Yea, that's the one, we've all been there.

This response made us both laugh, but more importantly what that response done was acted as a circuit breaker, acknowledging the response allowed the body to regulate, laughter allowed the nervous system to soften, and the crying passed through with a wave and a "see ya later", the client stopped crying, his body language relaxed and we moved through the episode.

# What's Normal to the Spider is Chaos to the Fly

**A lesson on embracing our differences, finding self-acceptance and reframing negative core beliefs we have dressed in over the years.**

I see people come through my counselling practice for many different reasons; a common reason being they feel different. People seek therapy for a myriad of presentations. It could be to address specific issue such as a relationship break down, anxiety, depression or a circumstantial issue they are struggling with. However, beneath these surface level concerns usually lies a deeper discomfort, a discomfort that can only be discovered through compassionate inquiry and holding space for the persons experience from a therapeutic lens. That discomfort is a core belief, and whatever the situation the client is facing has wounded and reaffirmed that individuals **core belief.** A core belief is a deeply ingrained belief that can shape our thoughts, attitude and behaviours. It is a fundamental belief that can influence how we see ourselves, others and the world around us.

Each person carries many core beliefs, core beliefs are formed in childhood, influenced by our upbringings and culture, they can be framed by our relationships, experiences, interactions and the script we or others have written for ourselves. Core beliefs are fundamental ideas individuals hold about themselves. These beliefs shape their perceptions, thoughts and behaviours, and when these beliefs are challenged or threatened, it can lead to distress, mental health dips and a strong desire to understand or change. Core beliefs can be positive or negative, they are subconscious and automatic, meaning that we may not always be aware of them or questions their validity, this is why exploring core beliefs with a therapist can be pivotal.

**Common core beliefs**

I am not worthy of love.

No one likes me.

I am different.

I do not deserve to be happy.

I am not good enough.

For example, if someone comes to therapy really struggling with the breakdown of a relationship, there may be more to the response that the loss of the relationship, of course break ups are sad and hard to come to terms with, but additionally a relationship ending may reaffirm a core belief that they are not worthy of love/not good enough or do not deserve to be happy. The impact of this can cause a lot of long-term emotional injury – this injury effects a person's self-esteem and self-worth causing all sorts of emotional, mental and sometimes behavioural issues.

Similarly, a person coming to therapy seeking help dealing with social anxiety, on the surface it may look like a fear of public speaking, fear of meeting new people or fear of rejection but underlying this surface issue could be a deep-rooted core belief such as "no one likes me" or "I am different". This belief will likely stem from an experience of rejection, abandonment, perhaps even a playground incident in the formative years. The emotional injury of this experience can leave a deep-seated fear of relational exchanges and insecurity in our relationships but more prominently that with ourselves. Through talking therapy, self-discovery and inner work we can all discover the core beliefs that we carry, simply bringing them into our awareness, reflecting reframing and reestablishing new core beliefs can promote healing, growth, and transformation, giving exposure to these anxieties and forming new experiences can help us form healthier relationships with ourselves and others.

In a world that often values conformity and tries to fit individuals into predefined boxes, (here I go again ranting about the education/societal system) it is essential to understand that is impossible to fit into a predefined box and even more important to recognise and accept our uniqueness. As the saying goes, "What's normal to the spider is chaos to the fly."

As aforementioned most of us have experienced the feeling of feeling different, sometimes described as on outside looking in, which can lead to self-doubt, anxieties, isolation and feelings of not being enough (hello core belief). However, the truth is that we are all different, and embracing our differences is not only normal but also absolutely brilliant.

Let's explore these societal expectations placed upon us, the struggles individuals face when feeling different, and how therapy and self-acceptance can help us navigate these common challenges.

## Society's Expectations and the Pressure to Conform

From a young age, society bombards us with expectations and standards of what is considered "normal." In the educational environment we are uniformed not only in our clothes but our behaviour and performances. But much like the albitites of the spider and the fly, we all have our strengths and capabilities some who don't conform to the academic curriculum, this is a conformity I personally massively and absolutely can relate too. I struggled in school, I couldn't focus and got bored easily, this likely was deflected by my rascally behaviour but rather than looking into the need some teachers deemed me as incapable, developed a core belief "I am stupid" please forgive that world as it's now a word I feel is non-existent but yes a teacher actually said those words to me, likely in front of a room full of others, they told me I was unremarkable and wouldn't amount to anything, all because I couldn't recite the periodic table. Today, I am so very grateful to that teacher, I did mention at the beginning of this book I had a rebellious streak? So, whilst I struggled with the core belief of my intellect, I did everything in my power to reframe that. In saying that I had some fantastic teachers too and I do look back on my school years with fondness, which just goes to show how one person can influence a person's self-belief. This works the other direction too by the way, it really does just take one person to have faith in us and help us achieve our potential, one person's belief can be a catalyst that propels us forward, I'm grateful to have so many people around me that have reframed this limiting belief, so be a cheerleader when you can. These expectations can shape our perceptions of ourselves and create a sense of pressure to fit in. Please understand that these societal norms are often arbitrary and do not define our worth or value as individuals, we are all beautifully unique, each bringing something different to the table and that is definitely something worth celebrating, who wants to party with robots anyway?

## The Feeling of Being Different

Feeling different can lead to feelings of alienation and inadequacy. This feeling can stem from various aspects, such as our appearance, personality traits, interests, or cultural background. It is crucial to acknowledge that being different is not a flaw but rather a unique aspect of our identity.

## Seeking Therapy for Feeling Different

Therapy can be a valuable resource for individuals who feel different and struggle with self-acceptance. Many people seek therapy to explore their feelings, gain insight into their experiences, and develop coping strategies. A therapist can provide a safe and non-judgmental space to discuss and navigate the challenges associated with feeling different. Don't be shy in reaching out for support, a common misconception of therapy is that it is used in crisis, no, therapy is a space for all, it is a space for not only healing but self-discovery.

## Affirmations for Self-acceptance

Affirmations can be a simple yet powerful tools that can help us embrace and accept ourselves fully and truly all whilst reframing the self-restricting thoughts and beliefs we limit ourselves with. Here are some affirmations that can support self-acceptance but do take some time to reflect on your own core beliefs creating some affirmations to soothe.

a. **"I am unique, and my differences make me special."**

b. **"I celebrate and honour my individuality."**

c. **"I am worthy of love and acceptance just as I am."**

d. **"I embrace my differences and use them to create positive change in the world."**

**e. "I am proud of who I am and the journey I am on."**

## Embracing Self-acceptance

Accepting we fully and truly requires self-compassion, resilience, and a commitment to personal growth. Here are some strategies to help embrace self-acceptance:

a. Practice self-compassion: Treat yourself with gentleness and compassion, acknowledging that everyone has strengths and weaknesses. When struggling with thoughts ask yourself what you would say to a friend experiencing similar. I doubt you would say to a friend what you are currently saying to yourself. Be kind.

b. Challenge societal norms: Question the societal expectations that make you feel inadequate and redefine success on your own terms.

c. Surround yourself with supportive people: Build a network of individuals who embrace and celebrate your differences, creating a sense of belonging.

d. Focus on personal growth: Engage in activities that align with your values and allow you to grow and flourish as an individual.

e. Celebrate your uniqueness: Embrace your quirks, talents, and interests, these are what make you who you are.

f. Recite and remind yourself what's normal to the spider is chaos for the fly, and that's what makes.

# Compassion is the Cure

**This passage explores how compassion can heal hearts and transform lives, starting from within.**

In life and as social beings seeking connection, we all have a natural desire to be seen and heard, however I feel it is more than that, I feel the need is to be held. And by held I don't mean in the literal sense although this is nice too when appropriate. When I talk of holding space for someone, I mean holding that person in compassion and empathy. Humans crave compassion. Firstly, compassion satisfies our need for belonging. Being met with compassion during our time of suffering is a powerful antidote to healing. In passage 1 we concluded that life is tough, with suffering being inevitable.

Sometimes the suffering of humans can be so terribly tragic that words aren't enough. Words of comfort and reassurance do not even begin to soothe the wound. In fact, words at times can give the opposite of comfort, for example, what do you say to a mother who has lost a baby? How do you begin to articulate that level of pain. There are no words that can comfort a mother whose arms are aching arms and heart is breaking in grief. When words aren't enough, offer compassion.

When we are met with compassion it not only validates our pain and the experience it offers practicalities, offering practical support in times of need comforts or reinforces safety in times of distress. Meeting someone with compassion can soften the feelings of loneliness, isolation and sadness that they are experience, it won't take away their pain, but it says, "I am with you, you are safe with me" and as we have already learnt two basic human needs are connection and safety.

In the early days of my career as a young inexperienced placement counsellor in a GP surgery I was refereed an elderly gentleman who had sadly lost his wife, his wife had passed away due to natural causes in the winter of life. The loss was colossal, he impact vast, married over 60 years this man's life changed dramatically, coupled with mourning the loss of his wife his feelings of safety and security were shook, the grief that followed was overwhelming. Husband and wife married young and only had each other, their story was a sad one, they lost their first child at a young age and in a bid to survive the magnitude of this lost they devoted their lives to one another. They even worked together setting up their own business. Naturally in this environment some level of co-dependency will form, a complex and devasting factor when it comes to bereavement. In some cases, co-dependency and bereavement can intersect. When a codependent individual loses their dependable or enabling relationship through death of the person, they were relying on it can intensify the grief and complicate the bereavement process. The loss of that person may activate extreme feelings of emptiness, confusion and even a loss of identity.

Now as a young therapist in training on a limited sessions timeframe where do I even begin to start with that. This was complex work and out of my capacity at this time, after some reflection, discussion with my wonderful supervisor we decided to contain the therapy within a person-centred approach whilst waiting on a referral for the relevant specialist services to reach out to client. One my first session with the client the client mentioned he couldn't bear to make tea, his wife had always made him his tea, his tea would be waiting on him when he got up each morning, ready for his arrival home and a pot put on before bed. The memory of his wife's tea caused a big emotional response and even an angry one. According to a structure pioneered by Swiss psychiatrist Elisabeth Kübler-Ross, there are five stages of grief. The five stages are – Denial. Anger. Bargaining. Depression and Acceptance. Of course we must remember these are part of a framework to help identify the feelings we are experiencing and each person experiences grief differently and on different timelines (there is that word different again.). In the session, I stayed with that emotion, inquiring how she made his tea and how it made him feel receiving the tea, this led to further stories of his wife spoke with fondness and tender memories shared to which the client got great comfort from.

When the client came to attend his next session, I had a cup of tea waiting ready for him. He simply thanked me for the tea, and we began our sessions.

The client attended for another 4 sessions and each week I had his tea ready for him. The signposted counselling slot opened, we ended our sessions, on our last he gave me a gift of a cup, at the time I didn't really understand the depth of his gift but was touched and thanked him none the less. Around a year later walking another client out I seen this client, he greeted me, and we got talking, he shared he was doing well and coming to terms with his grief, quipping he even made his own tea now! He ended our conversation by thanking me and told me the tea meant more to him than I'll ever know. I was surprised he had remembered.

Compassion comes in many forms, sometimes it's a hand on the shoulder or offer of a trip to the shop, a listening ear, or talking to the person that everyone is talking over, its noticing that someone doesn't seem themselves and inquiring to their wellbeing. It's helping a mother struggling to carry their shopping and manage their child or helping a pensioner across the road. Sometimes it is as basic as a cup of tea.

But in whatever form compassion has the potential to bridge the gaps, heal hurt and hold another human in their time of need.

**Choose compassion. Always.**

# Walls of Purpose

**A short teaching on finding purpose in our daily lives.**

Have you ever been to Ireland? If you've ever visited or plan to visit Ireland, you will notice many stone brick walls peppered randomly through the Irish countryside, these stone walls lead nowhere and contain nothing. The walls are around 8ft high and can be up to 300 yards long but vary in dimension. They serve little practical purpose. To an observer it may seem that these random walls in fields have no purpose whatsoever, the ironic thing is, that is exactly their purpose. **Purpose.**

In mid 19th century Ireland suffered a famine, this led to men losing their jobs, which in turn resulted in many men falling into a deep depression. In a bid to support the men through the depression local churches and landlords came up with the idea to build these walls, now referred to as famine walls, the idea behind the famine walls was to give a sense of purpose and dignity to the town folk, the men could go out to work each day and rather than have to beg or relay on charity handouts from those more fortunatc thcy could carn them, the men were paid in small sums and food. Ingeniously, there was much more to it than that, the actual labour of the work provided men exercise, community and more important purpose, all essential ingredients for promoting good mental health and wellbeing.

Purpose is crucial for mental health as it provides a sense of direction, meaning and fulfilment. All of which feels compromised in times of low mood or uncertainty. Having a clear direct purpose gives us something to strive for, a reason to get up each day and can even be a crutch of survival. When we have purpose, we feel more future focused, motivated and resilient. It can help us establish a strong sense of self, stability our identity and self-worth. Moreover, a purpose provides a sense of belonging and connection. When we have purpose each day, we will likely form connections around that purpose or form a network with likeminded people. This can provide further support and a sense of comradery. Again, all of which are essential to promoting good mental health. It provides a framework for how you want to live or spend each day; it is intertwined with your values and interests.

Purpose does not have to be enlightening or spiritual, purpose can be as simple as having a task to complete each day, it can be a soft goal to work towards or doing a chore. Finding joy in everyday moments or pursuing activities or actions that make you feel good. It could be visiting a friend or going to the gym.

Often when discussing purpose, people deep it, automatically considering what is the purpose is of their life. We all have much purpose to life. Your life purpose is simple, it consists of the central motivating aim of your life each day – the reason you get up each morning.

# Human Being or Human Doing

**Are you a human being or a human doing? This thought-provoking question invites us to reflect on our priorities, values and how we conduct our lives and schedules.**

In today's busy world we are conditioned to always be doing. The capacity we live is fast paced, it is overachieving with high levels of productivity and expectations. This coupled with the added conjecture of social media, we are often witness to the insatiable endeavours, accomplishments and seemingly success of our peers, thus adding additional pressure fuelling our need to be "doing" more. To navigate this challenging landscape, it's crucial to prioritise our well-being and develop strategies to manage stress effectively bur more importantly becoming aware of our own capacity, need to do and ability to just be.

Human biology did not evolve to cope with the level of pressure and stress that comes with the modern world. Our biological makeup developed over thousands of years, has been shaped by the challenges and environments our ancestors faced. However, the fast-paced, high-pressure nature of today's society can often exceed our natural capacity to cope and effectively handle the high levels of function we undertake in our day to day, due to this factor we are simultaneously contending with both over and under stimulation which can lead to stress, anxiety and symptoms of overwhelm.

**Let's expand on this**

In the past, our ancestors' primary concerns were survival-related: finding food from the land, shelter in nature and protection from predators. Their stress responses were triggered in situations that directly threatened their physical well-being. These stress responses, known as the "fight or flight" response, were crucial for their survival.

Fast forward to the present day, and our stressors have evolved significantly. We now face complex challenges such as work deadlines, financial pressures, social expectations, information overload and over exposure to the world we live in, the good, the bad and the ugly. That is a lot to process. Our bodies, however, have not evolved at the same pace to effectively cope with these modern stressors. When we experience stress, our bodies release hormones like cortisol and adrenaline, which prepare us for action. In small doses, these stress hormones can be beneficial, helping us focus and respond to the situation at hand. However, chronic or excessive stress can have detrimental effects on our physical and mental well-being. The constant pressure to perform, meet expectations, and juggle multiple responsibilities can lead to burnout, anxiety, depression, and various physical health issues. Burn out is a common issue presented in therapy. Our bodies may struggle to find balance and recover from the ongoing stress, leading to a state of chronic stress that takes a toll on our overall health, at times manifesting in physical illness.

It is important to consider the impact that modern lifestyle and the daily choices we make have on our biology. Factors such as sedentary behaviour, poor nutrition, lack of sleep, our busy lives and the constant exposure to screens and technology which can further exacerbate the effects of stress on our bodies and minds. In today's fast-paced world we are expected to have it all and do it all. This is impossible, the standards set by society are impossible to maintain without consideration to our wellbeing, boundaries and self-care. It is vital for our wellbeing to take time to rest, pause and just be still, detox from the digital world, make time for sensory respite, stress relief and moments of repose.

**Reflections**

I ask you again to consider this question; "Are you a human being or a human doing?' Exploring this question can be a thought-provoking exercise, here are some journalling prompts to consider.

1. **Reflect on your daily activities. Do you prioritise being or doing?**
2. **Why do you feel that is?**
3. **How does it feel to just be?**
4. **Do you associate any core beliefs with this state?**

5. **Reflect on the balance in your life.**
6. **Are there any adjustments you could make to create a healthier equilibrium?**

Take time to reflect on your answers, consider your stressors and symptoms of overwhelm, as well as coping mechanisms to help alleviate these symptoms.

**So, what exactly does it mean to "Just be"?**

Being is a state. A state presence and mindfulness, it is to be fully engaged in the moment we are experiencing, without being caught up in thoughts of the past or distracted with concerns for the future. It is to show up for us as we are, listen to the needs of our body and meet those needs, regardless of what expectations of external factors.

As we live in the modern world each of us will have non-negotiable commitments to tend to, therefore I am not suggesting you break these commitments or should have the ability to hit the pause button on life. Rather, I am asking you to meet yourself where you are, develop self-awareness and practice mindfulness whilst continuing with your life. I am suggesting comfort breaks throughout your day, saying no when things become too busy, managing your capacity and taking time to pause and process what is happening for you right now.

Being is a feeling. It is feeling inner calm and balance. Sitting with our feelings and experiencing mindful moments and regulation.

When you are in a state of being, you return to your authentic state. Feeling calm and present. Your mind becomes quiet, and you can observe what is going on around you rather than absorb it. You respond to situations rather than react. How peaceful does this sound? Being in this state can also enhance your ability to notice what is going on around you, manage challenges from a calmer perspective and feel more connected to yourself and others.

By reframing our understanding of the pressures, we face in the modern world and taking proactive steps to manage stress, we can better align our biology with our current environment. Sometimes that is simply slowing down, practicing mindfulness and just being as we are. In modern society it is easy to get caught up in what we "should" be doing. This can be influenced to what we see others doing and let's be honest we are all overexposed to the lives of others.

Do we ever pause to consider this influence? Is this what I really want or do I feel I should do it because I see so many others? The use of the word "should" could imply that our decisions or desires are imposed by others. I feel the word "should" reflects external influences, societal norms or the latest trend that we feel compelled to engage in.

Explore with adapting your language, swap "should" with "could" and take the pressure of. Could represents a sense of freedom, autonomy and choice, it defines that we have options and possibilities, allowing us to make our own decisions based on our wants.

How would it feel to consider that perhaps the key to success isn't always about the doing, perhaps the key to success is simply the art of just being, just maybe achievement is in the feeling of contentment and ease with where we are in life right now?

A limiting belief that many people carry is that rest is unproductive, that rest should be earned. It is also a common misconception that being stagnant in life is being unsuccessful, but what if, just for now stagnation is, ok? What if stagnation is contentment and you are exactly where you need to be at this present moment. What a freeing thought.

Reframe the need to "do" and appreciate the need to "be". Again, it can be helpful to adapt language here, so, rather than asking yourself what you need to do today, ask yourself how you need to be, meet yourself where you are, be present, consider your needs from an internal perspective.

**Here are a few suggestions to help live more presently.**

## Coping mechanisms for conscious living

### 1. Connect with nature

Take a walk or sit in a spot of natural beauty taking in the surroundings, observe what is around you, really tapping into each of your senses. Notice what you can see? What do you hear? What do you smell? How does the ground feel below you? How are you experiencing your surroundings? How does your body feel right now?

**2. Detach from your electronics**

Put the phone or laptop away, consider structured times to check correspondence or social media etc. Take time out daily from the digital world, perhaps consider a regular digital detox. It is recommended not to check social media one hour prior to bed or waking up.

**3. Consciously observe your thoughts and feelings**

Consider what messages your body is sending you, e.g. if you feel tired your body may be asking you to rest, really explore that feeling; how would exercise feel right now? Alternatively, how would it feel to sit down with a coffee or a book? Invite yourself to meet your needs.

**4. Reduce distractions**

Most of us are never fully present as we are continually getting distracted or attempting to complete too many tasks at once, therefore set time aside for each task. Make a list in priority order of what needs done, if a thought comes into your mind of another task to complete, do not stop your task to respond to the thought, simply add it to the list.

So be present, live in the moment, be gentle with yourself, take time to just be, the moment, be you, you are.

# A Soft Place to Land

**A narrative exploring the importance of tenderness within the therapeutic space.**

Each person's therapeutic process will be completely unique, as will be their stories, human experience and needs. With that in mind the tactic I deliver in the therapy room (and in life) is exclusive, it will vary from client to client, I offer a bespoke approach to therapy, tailored to the individual needs of each client, this is built around the client's unique personality and presentation. However, there is one core approach I will always provide, and that is soft.

## Softness is the core of my work

I have come to realise the immense importance of being gentle with my clients and those I engage with as a whole. Doing the work I do I am well informed that life, with all its challenges and hardships, can often leave individuals feeling battered and worn. When confronted with adversity and hardships, it is essential to find a gentle refuge, to seek solace and regain our strength. Many people seek therapy in a state of vulnerability. It is during these moments that therapy becomes a sanctuary, offering them a soft place to land. A soft place to land can be a remedy for healing and recovery.

As a therapist, I feel it is my assignment to create an environment of warmth, understanding, and compassion. I recognise that my clients may be carrying heavy burdens, it is my alliance to offer solace and respite from the outside world, propose a gentle presence, provide a safe space to lower their defences, and let down their guard. In this gentle space, I encourage clients to explore their emotions at their own pace. Holding space for the moment. I do not rush or push them to confront their pain before they are ready. Instead, I hold space for their vulnerability, allowing them to express themselves without judgment or criticism. Offer a listening ear, a compassionate heart, and a genuine desire to understand their experiences and sometimes simply a cup of hot tea and a place to rest.

In moments of distress, I remind my clients that it is okay to be gentle with themselves. I encourage self-compassion and self-care as essential tools for navigating life's challenges. Together, we explore gentle practices such as mindfulness, relaxation techniques, and self-soothing strategies that can provide comfort and support during difficult times. I wish to offer these reminders to whoever is reading right now. Be tender.

Being gentle in therapy also means recognising and respecting the unique journey of everyone. I understand that what works for one person may not work for another. I adapt my therapeutic approach to meet the needs and preferences of my clients, honouring their autonomy and empowering them in their healing process. I feel this is paramount protective factor outside the therapy room too, it is essential to adapt and meet our own needs each day, for what we needed yesterday, may not apply today.

Through gentle guidance and unconditional support, my aim is to instil hope in my clients. Life may be hard, but the therapy room or any place that feels safe and soft, can be a refuge amidst the storm. A place to find solace, gain clarity, and develop the strength to face challenges with resilience and grace.

In the gentle space of therapy, we offer comfort and empowerment for clients. I believe in their inherent worth and their capacity for growth and healing and remind clients of their brilliance often. Take this for yourself, remind yourself often of your brilliance, for its true, we are all extraordinary. By offering them a soft place to land, I hope to help them navigate life's complexities with kindness, understanding, and a renewed sense of hope.

As a therapist, I am privileged to witness the incredible resilience and strength of the human spirit. Every day, I have the remarkable opportunity to guide individuals on their unique journey towards healing and self-discovery.

One such client who stands out in my mind is a past client, Emily.

When Emily first entered my office, I could sense the weight she carried on her shoulders. Her eyes held a mixture of pain, fear, longing for relief and a need to understand and be understood. It was clear that she had been through significant hardships and was in desperate need of support.

With empathy as my compass, I created a safe and nonjudgmental space for Emily to explore her emotions and share her story. I listened intently, acknowledging the depth of her pain and validating her experiences. I understood that healing begins with feeling seen and heard, and I made it my priority to provide that for Emily. Due to the hardships Emily faced, this was having a physical impact on her body, she was tired, mentally, emotionally, physically and spiritually.

Through our sessions, I encouraged Emily to delve into her emotions and confront the underlying traumas that had shaped her life. It was not an easy process, as she had built walls of self-protection to shield herself from further pain. However, with gentle guidance her, helping her navigate through the layers of her past and unravel the patterns that held her back.

As our therapeutic relationship grew, Emily began to trust me and felt safe enough to peel back the layers of her vulnerability. She shared her deepest fears, insecurities, and darkest moments with me. In those moments, I realized the immense responsibility I held as her therapist, and I vowed to hold space for her pain and support her in her journey towards healing.

There were moments when Emily faced overwhelming emotions that threatened to consume her. She felt lost, as if she would never find her way out of the darkness.

In those moments, I provided a steady presence, a beacon of hope, reminding her that healing takes time and that she was not alone in her struggles.

Together, we explored various therapeutic techniques and coping strategies that would help Emily regain control over her life. We worked on building her resilience, nurturing self-compassion, and cultivating healthier ways of relating to herself and others. It was a collaborative process, and I marvelled at Emily's courage and determination to confront her pain and grow from it.

Over time, Emily's wounds began to heal, and I witnessed her transformation into a resilient and empowered individual. She reclaimed her sense of self-worth and discovered her true potential.

Emily's story serves as a reminder of the transformative power of therapy. It reaffirms my belief that every individual has the capacity to heal and grow, given the right support and guidance. As a therapist, I am honoured to walk alongside my clients, witnessing their strength and resilience as they navigate their path towards self-discovery and emotional well-being.

# The Art of Empathy
# – the gift of healing

**The art of empathy is the art of understanding, it is the art of being present with another person's pain, aligning with their experience. In this passage we will explore the importance of empathy in fostering genuine connection with other.**

It is a common misunderstanding that sympathy and empathy come hand in hand, but I believe they are too very different offerings. So, what's the difference?

While they are both related to understanding they, both differ in their response and level of involvement. Merely sympathy is expressed, it is the act of showing concern for someone's emotions rather than feeling them. Sympathy can be expressed in our actions or words, it usually involves offering support or words of comfort to others in their time of suffering e.g., "I am so sorry for your suffering, is there anything I can do?" you are understanding their problem and accepting that it is an issue for them, you are willing to help make sense of the problem, perhaps providing words of comfort, a different perspective or offerings of practical help. But yet you stand outside of the issue, as sympathy does not necessarily require understanding their emotions from their perspective.

Empathy, on the other hand is to experience the person's pain with them, it is the ability to fully understand and share those feelings, it is being fully present human to human siting together through their suffering, holding space for their experiences, with no judgement, no offering of another perspective, the ability to understand exactly how that person is feeling at that time. You stand inside that moment of pain with them.

Empathy is, at its simplest, a deep awareness and emotional connection to the emotions of other people. Empathy is the capability to fully connect with another human, to attune to their feelings, to experience their experience alongside them and see it exactly through their lens, as a therapist I have held space for many clients through their suffering, this to me is a privilege. I have learnt over the years of my therapeutic work in times of suffering, people do not want to hear how to fix it, they do not want to hear solutions or suggestions, or words of comfort such as e.g. "at least" what they need is for their feelings to be gently held and their story to be wholly heard, of course words of wisdom and phrases of comfort have their place however, when someone is deep in their pain, it can be healing to offer compassion rather than comfort, and empathy rather than sympathy. Empathy and compassion combined are potent healers. They foster connection and alleviate suffering, by offering empathy we create a positive ripple effect, essential antidotes to a disconnected and divided word. I believe that demonstrating empathy is a gift of healing.

"Empathy is the most precious human quality." Dalai Lama.

# Paving the Path to Inner Contentment

**Tips and techniques to lay the foundations of inner peace, presence and contentment.**

## What is inner contentment

Inner contentment is the acceptance of who you are, to embrace what you have and where you are in life at any given moment. Inner contentment is the ability to live peacefully and presently fully in control of your internal emotional state regardless of outside external factors. Contentment is the cornerstone to living a life in peace, harmony and balance. Possessing inner contentment can also reduce your stress level, promote wellness, develop a growth mindset and positive outlook towards life, making life more pleasurable. For me, to live contently is to live in freedom: a freedom to be who you are, enjoy who you are, and live life exactly as you are in that moment, without worrying about the future or fretting over the past. To live in the now. Each person will feel and view contentment differently, for some contentment may come in achieving milestones and personal goals. For others it may stem from finding inner peace and happiness in the present moment regardless of external factors. Contentment can be found in the simple pleasures of life; it can also be found in the big moments. Ultimately, contentment is a subjective experience that will vary from person to person, be shaped by their own individual values, beliefs and experiences. It is a deeply personal journey towards fulfilment and satisfaction.

Having inner contentment means you are not reliant on people, material things, external factors, or life circumstances to bring you fulfilment or give you comfort. You do not seek happiness from other sources that yourself or rely on others for happiness. Possessing a strong sense of inner contentment can help you make the best of our life regardless of where you find yourself. When you've developed a strong sense of inner contentment, your outlook in life is not easily shook or changed by what's happening in your environment. For example, someone with inner contentment could find themselves in a tough situation, however they will make the best of what is there, whereas if you have internal discontentment, you could be in the best circumstances and still find dissatisfaction.

## The journey to contentment

Contentment isn't a destination, it's a journey, it's a journey you will go through your entire life and as during any journey there may be obstacles along the way, wrong turns or diversions, the key is just to continue the path, keep pushing though developing our mindset along the way. As humans we are painfully aware that life is full of ups and downs, inner contentment will not stop the trials and tribulations of life, however it will help you overcome each and get through troublesome times in resilience and greater ease. It is human nature to catastrophise situations with the outcome to prepare for them, this can be the brains way of protecting our body from emotional pain or suffering, however I feel it amplifies our suffering, causing us to suffering twice. Sometimes causing us to suffer for no reason, as perhaps the thought of our suffering is more distressing than if/when the actual cause of our suffering occurs.

Being content is also having the awareness to know how to enjoy the ups and learn from the downs. Owning this internal protective factor can help one lead a life with less unnecessary suffering, to let go of what has been and the need to control of what is to come. It involves both surrender and gratitude and allows you to accept "what is" without the despair of holding onto "what could have been".

## Paving the path to contentment

Contentment may be very personal to everyone therefore I suggest you spend some time in self-reflection considering what contentment is personally to you, consider how it feels when you are content. How does your body feel? What is the overriding emotion you associate with contentment? How does life look? What is contentment to you? Think of a time you felt contented. How did this feel?

Once you have sourced your internal response to contentment you may wish to follow these simple suggestions to get your started on the road to cultivating contentment, it may be an idea to develop some of your own, based on your own personal discovering.

## Steppingstones to contentment

### Develop an attitude of gratitude

Gratitude is more than saying thank you, it is developing a deep appreciation for life and the world around you, it is looking at life with a positive appreciation, considering what you have rather than what you would like. Make a commitment to practice gratitude. Each day identify at least one thing that enriches your life, regularly acknowledge the feeling of gratitude when it surfaces.

### Live in the moment

Don't postpone happiness by waiting for a day when your life is less busy or less stressful. That day may never come. Live now. Enjoy the small pleasures of life. If you struggle to see those pleasures create them. Implore one act daily of something you enjoy, this should be something you don't have to do, instead set a daily intention of something you wish to do. T

his could be as small or extravagant as you like. The only stipulation is to do it regularly.

### Let go of the need to control

Recognise what you can or cannot control. You will soon find that there is very little we can control in life. Of course, we can concern ourselves over external contributors, however, there is little we can do to control them. What we can control is our reactions and actions. Work on your own reactions, the rest will work out.

To be content does not mean you do not desire more or wish to live a fuller life, it simply means you are thankful for life as it is now and patient for what is to come. **Live presently, learn often, laugh more and love much,** follow these steps, **believe in yourself** and you are halfway there.

# Anxiety – Friend, or Foe?

**Anxiety is a natural human response to the world around us, every person will experience anxiety at some point in their week. Embracing our anxiety can act as a friendly guide to growth and personal development.**

**What exactly is anxiety?**

Anxiety is the mind and body's reaction to stressful, dangerous, unfamiliar or even familiar situations. It's the sense of uneasiness, distress, or dread you feel before a significant event or during a particular stressful situation. Anxiety can present in many forms, many sufferers will experience the physical effects of anxiety, feeling that nervous energy consume the body. Others however may develop cognitive issues due to anxiety, developing unhelpful thinking styles, such as catastrophising, overthinking, or create negative thought patterns.

Anxiety is a part of day to day live. If I was to blindfold you and ask you to run across the motorway your body would automatically feel anxious, right? This is your body telling you something is not right and to proceed with caution.

If we become aware of anxious moments, we will soon recognise it is a feeling we experience regularly, a feeling that sometimes passes quickly, a certain level of anxiety helps us stay alert and aware, keeping us safe or warning us of danger but for those suffering from an anxiety disorder, it feels far from normal - it can be completely debilitating, at times becoming overwhelming, life limiting and somewhat damaging to our confidence. Problematic anxiety can directly affect the way you think and behave. You may not even be aware of this happening. Psychological symptoms include Feeling worried, tense, or fearful for no obvious reason. Mood swings, lack of motivation and concentration. Overthinking and negative thought patterns. - Everyone experiences anxiety differently. There are lots of symptoms. It can also present with physical symptoms, such as heart palpitations, tummy pains or headaches. Some people know their anxiety is triggered by a specific fear, while plenty more find that they're anxious for no apparent reason. It's important to act if you notice signs of anxiety. Leaving them untreated can mean they get worse and lead to further health problems. Avoiding your triggers result in deeper secondary levels of anxiety, therefore it is best to acknowledge these feelings with the aim to explore, understand and address the message the body is sending you.

The thing is anxiety can appear when we least expect it, just like an old friend delivering a message to us. When presented with anxiety in the counselling space many people will share with me, they are anxious, but they don't know why, they are frustrated that they cannot work out where it is coming from Many people spend their energy trying to understand the cause of the anxiety rather than looking at the cure. When experiencing feelings of anxiety first and foremost it is best to explore the sensations of anxiety, using techniques and coping mechanisms to manage and soothe these feelings.

## Case Study

### Jacob age 19 - Presentation – Anxiety

Jacob came to counselling as he was struggling with anxiety, he described the anxiety as overwhelming – rating it an 8/10 – Jacob mentioned he rarely felt anxious and had a great life, was happy in himself, everything around him was going well, he had even started a new job which he really enjoyed. Then one day out of nowhere he experienced daily crippling fear, paranoid thoughts and feelings of self-consciousness, he just couldn't understand where these feelings were coming from, it felt totally out of his control, he struggled to make sense of it. We began our work by sitting with the feelings Jacob experienced, exploring the thoughts he was having and learning coping skills to manage when things became overwhelming. As the weeks progressed Jacob felt his anxiety lessoning. Each week Jacob shared how his week had gone, addressed his fears which naturally led to touching on some past experiences. We spoke of previous experiences Jacob had faced in life. Jacob went back into his childhood sharing both fond and adverse childhood experiences. Whilst touching on his primary school years Jacob shared a story of his first day in Primary 1 – he was around 5 and recalled an incident that resulted in Jacob accidently being locked in a storeroom, as he revisited this childhood memory he began to feel panicked, stating his anxiety was spiking, as we explored this memory deeper Jacob had a visceral response to the memory, we worked through the response gently holding space, compassion and consideration for the response and experience, staying with it until his anxiety softened. Once Jacob had come out of the memory, he was able to identify part of his job in his new workplace was conducted in a small storeroom similar to the one from his school experience, through delving deeper and exploring therapeutically he was able to link his anxiety back to the traumatic experience he encountered in his formative years. This helped Jacob understand the response which in turn allowed him to regulate his anxiety and use coping mechanisms to overcome anxious feelings.

## Let's break it down

When a traumatic memory is triggered, it can activate anxiety in the body through the complex interaction between the neurological and nervous system responses. Here's a short explanation of how this process occurs:

**Stage 1. Traumatic Memory:**
Traumatic memories are stored in the brain's limbic system, particularly the amygdala, which is responsible for emotional processing. These memories are often associated with intense fear, helplessness, or threat.

**Stage 2. Triggering Event:**
A triggering event, such as a specific sight, sound, smell, or even a thought, can activate the traumatic memory. This event can be like the original traumatic experience or simply remind the individual of the trauma.

**Stage 3. Amygdala Activation:**
When a triggering event occurs, the amygdala quickly evaluates the situation for potential threats. If the amygdala perceives the triggering event as a threat, it sends distress signals to various parts of the brain and body.

**Stage 4. Neurological Response:**
The amygdala activates the hypothalamus, which triggers the release of stress hormones like adrenaline and cortisol. These hormones prepare the body for a "fight-or-flight" response by increasing heart rate, blood pressure, and respiration.

**Stage 5. Nervous System Response:**
The autonomic nervous system, specifically the sympathetic nervous system, is activated in response to the stress hormones. This leads to physiological changes, such as dilated pupils, increased sweating, and muscle tension, preparing the body to react to the perceived threat.

**6. Anxiety Response:**
The combined neurological and nervous system responses can result in feelings of anxiety. The individual may experience a sense of impending danger, restlessness, racing thoughts, and heightened emotional arousal.

It's important to note that traumatic memories and the resulting anxiety response can vary from person to person. Some individuals may develop post-traumatic stress disorder (PTSD), which involves persistent re-experiencing of the traumatic event and significant impairment in daily functioning. Seeking professional help, such as therapy or counselling, can be beneficial in managing traumatic memories and anxiety.

## Nervous System Regulation

Our nervous systems are the primary centre for our bodies, it regulates all our programs and controls how we experience the world around us. When are nervous system feels safe and secure, we too feel safe and secure. The nervous system is so intelligent it can also respond to our external world, responding to the people we meet, the activates we do, the situations we find ourselves in. It is extremely complex and comes in two forms – the central and parasympathetic. The parasympathetic nervous system is responsible for the body's rest and safety responder, it basically checks in to keep us safe and sends messages to the body.

When the nervous system becomes dysregulated due to distress or prolonged feelings of stress it can lead to prolonged state of anxiety, worry, trouble sleeping and various other problematic internal responses. I feel nervous system health is extremely important to maintain good mental health and nervous system regulation can be a key factor to healing.

There are many therapeutic techniques that a person can use to regulate their parasympathetic nervous system causing a relaxion response within the body, this can counteract the body's stress response, allowing us to soothe and settle any negative feelings we may be experiencing. However, using the breath to regulate is the most accessible. Here's a simple breathwork technique to use to regulate when you feel overwhelmed or stressed.

**Breathing Technique**

Simply breathe deeply though your nose, release through your mouth, repeat until soothed. Some people find it helpful to repeat an affirmation with each breath they take, this can be tailored to the feeling, e.g., if you feel dysregulated due to a fear response, repeat, "I am safe" alternatively, it can be beneficial to focus on a comforting word or calming visual.

**Befriending anxiety.**

There is no doubt about it, that anxiety will be present in your week. It's a natural feeling we all have, it can at times be a positive emotion, if managed. Should anxiety persist or become unmanageable it is best to seek professional help.

If managed well anxiety keeps us safe, telling us that something is up. It is our protector. It is our guide. It can be our friend. For example, if I was to blindfold you and ask you to cross the motorway, your automatic response would be to feel anxious right? Our internal bodyguard kicks in, it isn't safe is the message delivered.

So next time you feel anxious really explore the feeling, hold space for it.

What is your body telling you? Are looking after yourself? Do you need to rest?

If the anxiety is present around particular people or situations, what is the message it wishes to send us.

Our body can be our greatest source of wisdom, it knows us more than anyone else, it knows our safety responses, our triggers, protective factors and when we are in need.

Trust it. Listen to it. Learn to align with its messages. Befriend it.

Here are some simple steps to manage & explore anxiety.

## Therapeutic Techniques

### Journaling - Writing down your thoughts can be a helpful therapeutic technique

It benefits anxiety in two ways.

First, journaling provides an opportunity to release thoughts - something that far too many people hold inside.

Second, writing down worries puts thoughts in a permanent place and tells your brain that it doesn't have to focus on remembering them as much.

**Breathing Techniques – the breath can regulate our central nervous system soothing the body and settling the mind**

Breathwork is our most accessible coping skill.

A simple breathing exercise is Box breathing, also known as four-square breathing, it involves exhaling to a count of four, holding your lungs empty for a four-count, inhaling at the same pace, and holding air in your lungs for a count of four before exhaling and beginning the pattern anew.

Some people find it helpful to make a square with their hand to follow as they do this exercise.

**Distraction - Acknowledge the anxiety and then move through it**

Consider embodied movement to release any pent-up energy, a gentle flow or a walk can help. Get creative, begin a creative task such as cooking, baking, drawing etc, it can be as simple as phoning a friend or going for a walk, the key is not to let the anxiety get the better of you. You've got his.

**Therapy or talk it out - hold space for your thoughts and feelings**

Talking things through in a safe comfortable environment with someone you trust, or a professional allows time for healing, giving you the space to process thoughts and make sense of feelings, understanding your needs will positively impact your life.

Remember, anxiety management is about helping your mind learn to cope with stress better so that the symptoms of anxiety aren't as severe.

Anything that promotes relaxation may be helpful.

Our bodies are our greatest tools. Learn to listen to your body, take your rest when you need it, look after yourself and make time for self-care.

You are stronger than any feeling, feelings are just temporary.

(Should feelings persist, seek professional help.)

# Don't Set Yourself on Fire to Keep Others Warm

**If you continue to set yourself on fire you will eventually burn out.**
**A lesson on boundaries, saying no and stepping away from people pleasing tendencies.**

In our society, often we glorify the act of selflessness and putting others before ourselves. While it is admirable to be caring and helpful, and of course necessary to be compassionate to other, constantly prioritising the needs of others at the expense of our own mental health and well-being can have detrimental effects. There is a huge difference between compassion and people pleasing. It is vital to know the difference between doing things for others because we 'want to" or doing it because we feel we 'need' to". This chapter explores the behaviours, feelings associated, impact and negative consequences of consistently doing things for others, providing gentle insights into the importance of self-care and establishing healthy boundaries.

## Behaviour - Neglecting Self

When we constantly focus on meeting the needs of others, we tend to neglect our own needs. We may say yes too often, when we don't have time or capacity which can lead to exhaustion, burnout, and a decline in overall mental health. Ignoring our own needs can have long-term consequences and hinder our ability to effectively support others in the long run. As the saying goes "You can't pour from an empty cup".

### Feeling - Resentment and Emotional Drain

Consistently putting others first without considering our own needs can lead to feelings of resentment and emotional drain. We may find ourselves feeling overwhelmed, emotionally exhausted, and unable to meet our own emotional needs. This can strain relationships and negatively impact our mental well-being. Constantly prioritising others' needs over our own can lead to low mood and a sense of diminished self-esteem. We may start to doubt our own worth and value, feeling that our needs are less important or not worthy of attention. This can have a significant impact on our mental health, leaving us feeling unfulfilled and emotionally depleted.

### Consequences - Boundary Erosion & stunting personal growth

Failing to establish and maintain healthy boundaries can result in a gradual erosion of our sense of self. We may find ourselves constantly accommodating others' requests and sacrificing our own desires and priorities. This can lead to a loss of personal identity, increased stress, and a diminished sense of self-worth. When we consistently focus on others, we may neglect our own personal growth. Our own goals and wellbeing take a backseat as we devote our time and energy to meeting the needs of others. This can result in a sense of stagnation and a loss of purpose.

## Impact - Co-dependency and unhealthy relationships

Constantly doing things for others can contribute to codependent patterns and unhealthy relationships. We may become overly reliant on others' approval and validation, seeking our sense of self-worth through their acceptance. This can create an imbalance in relationships and perpetuate unhealthy dynamics.

While it is important to be caring and supportive, constantly putting others first without considering our own needs can have detrimental effects on our mental health and overall well-being. It is essential to prioritise self-care, establish healthy boundaries, and recognize the importance of our own needs and desires. By taking care of ourselves, we can better support and help others in a sustainable and healthy way. Remember, self-care is not selfish; it is a vital component of wellness.

## What are boundaries and how do we establish them?

Having clear, concise and consistent boundaries is essential in maintaining a balanced lifestyle and healthy relationships. Boundaries are a form of self-protection, self-preservation and self-care. Boundaries can be set around any aspect of our life from relational boundaries, professional boundaries and content boundaries. Basically, all elements of our life should have boundaries, these are the line we draw or the limits we set to keep ourselves healthy and live a life aligning to our core values. For example, a personal boundary in a relationship can be how emotionally close you let people get to you, or how much you share about your life with this person, boundaries can vary from person to person depending on how "safe" the relationship is from your lens. Boundaries are also where you draw a line within the relationship, limit contact or cut it altogether. It can be necessary to put up boundaries in a relationship that may be detrimental to your mental health or relational hurt repeatedly occurs within the relationship. Perhaps a friend gossips about you or tells others personal information you would rather they didn't, in that case a boundary would be to keep the chat surface level and not confide too much in that person.

Professional boundaries are the limits you set around career/working life, i.e. the workload or timeframe you set yourself to meet work goals, again, this is necessary for maintaining a good work life balance, an example of a boundary could be not to take work calls while spending time with the family or have a cut-off point to answering emails etc, in today's busy world we are often fully accessible, working boundaries are key in maintaining healthy work life balance.

Content boundaries is the restriction to amount of the life content we expose ourselves too, content that perhaps needs managed to maintain a healthy lifestyle or promote good mental health, for example we may limit social media or screen time, setting a boundary to avoid or deactivate our apps at weekends or mornings etc. It can be necessary to have content boundaries around unhealthy content such as takeaways, alcohol or spending. Boundaries are super personal and should meet your own personal needs and align with your own core values.

**Tips for healthy boundaries**

1. **Reflect on your core values, work out what your deal breakers are, give some thought to what you expect from your relationships. Establish boundaries accordingly.**

2. **Consider your capacity when it comes to work life. Notice what aspects of work you become overwhelmed around? Lay down some structured boundaries around this.**

3. **Identify the regular content of your lifestyle that could be problematic in your life, most content is ok in moderation, however, too much of anything can become unhealthy. What content do you specifically struggle with? Set limits and stick to them.**

The key to maintaining boundaries lies in consistency, when we are consistent in our boundaries, we have a clear framework to follow, others will also be clear of our needs. Having boundaries is not a selfish act, it is a necessary act, strong boundaries promote healthy relationships but most importantly it promotes good self-esteem and self-worth.

# How to Hug a Hedgehog

**A creative tale on navigating the difficult people in our lives.**

We all have people in our day to day lives who can be difficult. They may be colleagues, neighbours or those a bit closer to home. This creative tale tells the story of a happy harmonious hedgehog called Harold, as he navigates life living beside prickly people. Through Harolds compassionate approach and unwavering warmth, he teaches his prickly pals how to embrace warmth and kindness. The story of Harold the Hedgehog can inspire us to see our peers through the eyes of compassion.

## Harold the Harmonious Hedgehog

There once was hedgehog named Harold. Harold had a unique ability to navigate through the thorny challenges and difficult situations that often arose in his life. His spiky exterior served as a protective shield, but beneath it, he had a heart full of warmth and understanding. Harold lived in a community of other hedgehogs, some of which did not share Harolds kind values, gentle nature and positive outlook. The garden the hedgehogs lived in was beautiful with lots of mealworms, crickets and beetles. There was plenty of greenery and soil to snuffle and dig, it was an ideal place for a happy hedgehog but unfortunately a new family of hedgehogs had recently taken residency in the garden, Harold found his new neighbours to be difficult and draining. Harolds new neighbours were often complaining, and regularly caused havoc in the garden, they seen everything as a negative and weren't too shy on voicing their opinions. The environment was a safe secure area that any hedgehog would be thrilled with, but not these guys, Harold struggled to understand it.

One sunny morning, Harold encountered a group of particular hedgehogs all who were known for their sharp tongues and prickly attitudes. They seemed to find joy in criticising others creating discord and had a very negative outlook on life. Everything was a problem to these hedgehogs, they complained regularly, gossiped and often downgraded others.

Intrigued by their behaviour, Harold decided to observe them closely in the hope of learning why the hedgehogs where like this. Harold just could not comprehend why a group of hedgehogs in this lovely garden could always be so miserable. As he watched their interactions, Harold noticed that these hedgehogs often reacted defensively at any encounter or communication. They would puff up their quills and lash out, causing conflict. Even the smallest of comments could set these guys into a rage. Harold soon realised that this defensive behaviour stemmed from their fear of being hurt or judged. Their need to gossip was a form of self-protection and their negative outlook a projection of their unhappiness. When Harold understood the depth of the hedgehog's pain, he felt saddened.

Determined to find a more harmonious environment for them all, Harold approached the group of hedgehogs with a gentle smile. He spoke softly, acknowledging their concerns and offering his understanding. He showed them that he was willing to listen without judgment, creating a safe space for them to express themselves.

Over time, Harold's compassionate approach began to dissolve the prickly barriers of the other hedgehogs. When the hedgehogs met Harold with aggression he met them with indifference, when faced with critic from the hedgehogs he responded with kindness.

Eventually it seemed the hedgehogs began to learn from Harolds harmonious ways. They softened their demeanour and even changed their communication style.

They started to open and share their vulnerabilities, realising that Harold genuinely cared about their well-being and the garden could be a more pleasant space to live. Slowly but surely, a sense of trust and respect began to grow among them.

Inspired by Harold's peaceful demeanour, the hedgehogs started to adopt his empathetic approach. They learned to embrace their own vulnerability and express their concerns in a more constructive and assertive manner. Thc oncc prickly atmosphcrc transformed into a supportive and nurturing environment. Through his journey, Harold taught us a valuable lesson in navigating difficult people in our lives. Just like hugging a hedgehog, it requires patience, understanding, and a willingness to see beyond the prickly exterior. By approaching others with kindness and empathy, we can create a space for growth, healing, and understanding, fostering meaningful connections even in the face of adversity.

# Just Another Mindful Monday

## How to make the week work for our wellbeing

It goes without saying we are conditioned to automatically have a negative mindset around Mondays, it is common to develop a moody Monday mindset which can even creep into our Sunday. Ever had the Sunday anxies? I think most of us can relate at some stage. Sunday anxies, is the anxiety we feel on a Sunday at the thought or dread of the week ahead. These feelings can be repetitive and form a negative loop that becomes part of our weekly routine. Having a negative outlook on a Sunday about the week ahead can bleed into the next day setting the tone for the week.

How would it feel to replace the Sunday anxies, with the concept of Self Care Sundays? What I mean by Self Care Sunday is rather than give into the anxiety or get caught up on dreading the week ahead, we could consciously prepare for the week to take some of the pressure of, incorporating self-care into your Sunday evening can make for a restful day or productive day rather than a day spent procrastinating or worrying – self-care Sunday could be anything from spending some time meditating or journaling to meal prepping or planning your outfits for the week, basically anything that will take the pressure of you either emotionally or practically. With a bit of self-awareness, structure and routine we could own the week by leaning into the structure and energy of each day. Statically energy levels peak by Tuesday and Wednesdays, we tend to feel good as we are back in routine etc, however, by Thursday it is common to feel drained and "ready for the weekend" as our bodies and minds are now craving a rest; with that in mind energy levels thus productively tend to be lower, therefore I strongly recommend introducing" Wellness Wednesdays" into your schedule. This brief "hump day" mental maintenance could have a profound positive impact on your mood and mental health, enabling you to carry out the rest of the week reducing the risk of emotional/mental overwhelm.

**Here's why**

Simply it will give you something to work towards each week, consciously knowing you have the reset and rest can help motivate the mind to work towards that, breaking up the long week.

**Here's how**

Set time aside each week for yourself, prioritise your needs, Do I need an hour, or do I need more? Schedule the time in your day, consider what those needs are? Do I need rest? Do I need support? Do I need movement? Assess how your body feels, listen and meet accordingly, i.e. if you feel tired take a time out, enjoy a long bubble bath or gentle mediation, curl up with an herbal tea. If you feel hyped up you might need to shake off excess energy, take a brisk walk while listening to music, or journal to let go of thoughts. There is deep comforting in knowing we have control of our own wellbeing, by scheduling in these small protective factors each week we are taking control, this is an empowering measure.

# Eat the Frog

**A simple phrase and technique to help readers improve productivity, reduce procrastination and get down to business.**

## What is prioritisation?

Procrastination is the art of \delaying something, putting a task off or at times totally avoiding it altogether, perhaps letting it sit until someone else does it or pushing it under the carpet, so no one does it at all. When we procrastinate, we give more energy to thinking about the task at hand rather than the energy to complete it. It makes absolutely no sense.

I believe that people can by usually be categorised into 3 groups.

## Thinkers. Talkers and Doers

## Take some time to consider which one are you?

First up the thinkers: They think a lot before doing things. Most of the time creating scenarios around the situation, analysing every aspect, and exploring every possible outcome, this can at times create fear, problems, or anxiety around the situation, which will sometimes lead to avoidance. They tend to more think about doing things, then in turn doing very little at all.

We then have the talkers; they talk a lot about what needs to be done. Spending more time discussing life rather than living it. It is natural for talkers to put a lot of focus on what others are doing or put pressure on themselves by comparing themselves to others.

Talkers may also lean on others for reassurance and lack assertiveness when making decisions.

Finally, we have the doers: They actively do things that they think and talk about, taking immediate action, with little consider about the outcomes. Doers can categorise failures as lessons and experiences therefore they look at life with a growth mindset.

These people **EAT THE FROG** every time – in other words just get it done.

Let's dissect it. (The lesson, not the frog!). The more we think about a task, the bigger the task becomes, the more problems we consider may arise when completing the task or excuses we create not to complete the task.

Before we know it, the task is so overwhelming, we develop negative thoughts or sometimes anxiety around it. It can weigh heavy on our minds, causing us to overthink or feel emotionally overwhelmed.

This is where the **EAT THE FROG** technique comes in.

**Eat The Frog** is perfect for anyone who struggles with procrastination, it's a simple helpful technique we can apply to daily life to improve peak productivity levels.

**Eating the frog** means to just do it, otherwise the frog will eat you meaning that you'll end up procrastinating the whole day just at the thought of eating the frog.

But once that one task is done, the rest of the day will be easier for you, you will build momentum, motivation, and a sense of accomplishment at the beginning of your day, helping you achieve what is needed early on.

Consider this, imagine I told you to eat a frog.

If you thought about it, you would be totally grossed out.

You would consider all the horrible textures and tastes that you would experience causing all sorts of negative thoughts and feelings around it. If you had to eat a frog it would be best to get this over an done with in the morning, right? Get it out of the way. Of course, it would as the thought of it would play heavily on your mind for the rest of the day causing all sorts of issues, basically putting off our tasks can have a similar detriment to our day.

This is where the **EAT THE FROG** technique comes in.

## Therapeutic Technique - EAT THE FROG

1. Identify your frog. Consider something you need to do, perhaps the task you most dislike for that day.

2. Do it first thing in the morning. Do not give yourself time to overthink it or put it off. Get it down.
3. Repeat this every day. This will have a positive impact on your mental health, overall wellbeing and improve productivity levels.

Give it a shot. A frog day keeps procrastination at bay.

# A Cactus Doesn't Live in the Dessert Because He Likes It

**A short creative story on how the wrong environment can promote or plummet our wellbeing.**

Mike was born in the dessert; he grew up there and knew life to be no other way. Although Mike felt great in himself, strong, firm and vibrant without pests or diseases just as a healthy cactus should. He felt curious about life outside the dessert. With no other cactus for miles, Mike often wondered what it would be like to have a companion or a friend to speak too. He began to get itchy feet, considering that there could be more to life than what the dessert had to offer.

Mike decided to leave his familiar home in search of a new and exciting adventure. With dreams of lush greenery and vibrant landscapes, Mike bid farewell to his hometown and set off on a journey to find a place where he felt he could truly thrive and curb his curiosity.

As Mike ventured beyond the desert, just as we do in this life of ours, he encountered many diverse environments - from the snowy mountains to the tropical rainforests. However, no matter where he went, Mike struggled to adapt. He noticed a dip in his mood, his strong form began to soften, and wither, he was often bothered by pests and spent a lot of energy fighting off disease. This drained Mike and he noticed his mood dip and energy plummet. Mike began to struggle.

In the snowy mountains, the cold temperatures froze his delicate roots, while in the rainforests, the excessive humidity made it difficult for him to breathe. Despite his best efforts, Mike realised that he did not belong here, and the climate just wasn't suited to his needs, no matter what Mike did to care for himself the environment was no good for him.

Feeling discouraged and out of place, Mike began to doubt his own uniqueness. He wondered why he couldn't flourish like the tall trees in the rainforest or the delicate flowers in the meadows. With slumped spines and thorns, Mike began the long road home, his mind filled with self-criticism and loathing. Mike blamed himself, he wondered was he not strong enough for these climates, what's wrong with me he questioned?

The thoughts and feelings became too much for Mike to handle, he needed some help overcoming the consuming feelings and intrusive thoughts he was experiencing. He sought an answer to his ruminating question of what is wrong with me? Mike remembered a wise saguaro cactus named Sage. On his journey home Mike stopped off to ask Sage for some insight into his experience, sharing his struggles and thoughts with the cactus.

Sage, with his weathered exterior and a heart filled with wisdom, listened attentively to Mike's struggles. He gently explained that each cactus and plant have its own purpose and environment in which it thrives and survives. Some plants may need warmer conditions other like a cool environment, even the level of watering various from plant to plant.

People are the same as plants. Each need different ways of nourishment and can thrive or wither depending on their environment. We don't expect our plants to thrive in all conditions. Yet we expect that from ourselves. You see, some people are like the sturdy cacti, thriving in the arid desert, while others are like delicate flowers, blooming in lush gardens. You see we all have specific environments to grow, both humans and plants have needs and preferences. All of which differ.

With Sage's guidance, Mike began to identify his needs and personal requirements understand that his uniqueness lay in his ability to survive and thrive in the harsh desert environment developing an awareness of his personal needs. He realised that his spines were not just for protection but also a symbol of his strength and resilience. Mike learned that true happiness and fulfilment come from embracing who you are and finding the environment where you can truly flourish.

Returning to the desert, Mike was welcomed back with open arms by his prickly companions. He shared his newfound wisdom with them, reminding them of the importance of embracing their own environments and celebrating their differences.

And so, the story of Mike, the brave cactus, teaches us that just as different plants thrive in different environments, people also have their unique strengths and talents, which are best showcased in environments that align with their true nature. It reminds us to embrace our individuality and respect the diverse environments in which we all thrive, for it is through this understanding that we can create a harmonious and flourishing world.

Moral of the story. A cactus doesn't live in the desert because it likes the desert; it lives there because the desert won't kill it. This simple observation holds a deeper truth about the relationship between living organisms and their environments. Just like the cactus, our environment plays a significant role in shaping our lives and overall well-being. What may be nurturing and uplifting for one person might be draining and suffocating for another. It is crucial to understand that our environment encompasses not only the physical surroundings but also the social, cultural, and emotional contexts in which we exist.

Let's delve into some examples of how our environment can influence our mental health. Imagine a person living in a crowded city, surrounded by noise, pollution, and constant hustle. While some individuals thrive in such an environment, finding energy and inspiration in the vibrant urban landscape, others may feel overwhelmed and anxious. The fast-paced lifestyle, lack of green spaces, and limited opportunities for solitude can take a toll on their mental well-being.

On the other hand, consider someone living in a serene countryside, surrounded by lush green fields and tranquillity. This environment might provide a sense of peace and calmness, allowing individuals to unwind and recharge. However, for some, the isolation and lack of social connections in such a setting may lead to feelings of loneliness and isolation.

These examples illustrate the importance of recognising when our environment is impacting our mental health negatively and when it is nurturing our well-being. It is crucial to become aware of the signs and symptoms that indicate the need for reassessing our surroundings.

Firstly, pay attention to your emotions and energy levels. Are you constantly feeling drained, anxious, or irritable? Do you find it challenging to concentrate or feel motivated? These could be signs that your environment is not meeting your individual needs.

Secondly, reflect on your physical health. Are you experiencing unexplained physical symptoms, such as headaches, stomach-aches, or sleep disturbances? Our environment can contribute to these symptoms and indicate that it is time for a change.

Lastly, consider the quality of your relationships. Are you surrounded by supportive and positive individuals who uplift you? How do you feel around the people you surround yourself with? Do you find yourself in toxic or unsatisfying relationships? Our social environment has a significant impact on our mental well-being, and it is essential to surround ourselves with people who contribute positively to our lives and make us feel good.

Becoming aware of these signs and symptoms is the first step towards reassessing our environment.

**Strategies**

**Here are some strategies to help you create a more conducive environment for your mental health**

**1. Identify your needs:**
Take the time to reflect on what you need from your environment to feel happy, fulfilled, and at peace. This could include aspects such as quiet spaces, access to nature, or opportunities for social interaction.

**2. Make changes:**
Once you have identified your needs, take steps to make necessary changes in your environment. This could involve finding a new living space, creating designated areas for relaxation and solitude, or seeking out social activities that align with your interests.

**3. Seek support:**
Don't hesitate to seek support from friends, family, or mental health professionals. They can provide guidance and help you navigate the process of reassessing your environment.

**4. Practice self-care:**
Engage in activities that promote your well-being and mental health. This could include exercise, mindfulness, hobbies, or spending time in nature.

Remember, just like the story of Mike the cactus, our environment can have a significant impact on our lives. By becoming aware of how our surroundings affect our mental health and taking proactive steps to create a supportive environment, we can nurture our well-being and thrive as individuals. Should you ever find your wellbeing compromised, consider your needs, question and assess the environment you find yourself in before questioning yourself, then you can assess a self-care plan or a way forward. Do not make the mistake Mike made in doubting himself.

# Teardrops on the Dancefloor

**In a world where happiness is often equated in our external behaviours is it is easy to assume that people aren't battling internal struggles. However sometimes a closer look can identify a different reality. In this passage we explore the paradoxical nature of partying through pain.**

The dance of life isn't easy and although it may look like everyone is having a good time sometimes all is not what it seems. How many times have you looked at others and assumed they were living their best life? Social media portrays an image that whoever is posting wants us to see, and sometimes this could not be further from the persons human experience. We see the perfectly curated picture, smiling faces and similarly carefree lifestyles and can't help but figure how happy that person must be. Often comparing our own lives to that moment, the person has created and chosen to share.

A phrase that I often refer to while explaining this paradox is "Teardrops on the dancefloor"

Let's circle back to my time in Ibiza. Obviously, a lot of time spent in Ibiza was spent clubbing and enjoying the vast night club the island had to offer. Ibiza is well known for its party vibes and club scene. The biggest club in Ibiza is Privilege. It is a well-known super club with the capacity to hold around 10,000 people, every night it was filled with partygoers and thrill seekers seeking escapism from reality. Privilege is renowned for its massive dancefloors, impressive stage production and world class DJ line ups, back then it was a staple of Ibiza night life attracting clubbers from all over the world. On walking into a club such as Privilege it may look like these 10,000 people are the happiest people in the world, and at the time I am sure they certainly feel this way, I know I did. The energy is high, and atmosphere is euphoric you can't help but absorb it, but what happens when the party is over? What goes up must come down right?

Well, the images you see on social media are similar.

What happened before, after and in-between that happy moment?

You see it is easy to assume that everyone is having the time of their lives. But beneath the surface of smiles and masks, many individuals hide their true emotions. This passage explores the concept of low mood and the emotional struggles that people conceal while on moving through the dance of life. The title "Tear Drops on the Dancefloor," illustrates the dichotomy between the external appearance and internal turmoil.

## The Dance of Concealment

As human beings, we possess a remarkable ability to repress and hide our emotions, even in the most public and social settings. It is often said that sometimes those who seem the happiness on the outside or don't discuss their thoughts and feelings are the ones who struggle most.

Mental health does not come with a bandage, unlike a physical fracture when our mental health is fragile, we don't tell others or may not have obvious symptoms or visuals to display our wounds. Just like on the dancefloor, individuals may be surrounded by friends, engaging in fun activities and laughter. However, behind the facade of fun and joy, there may be a torrent of emotions that remain unseen. Tears may silently fall amidst the pulsating beats, hidden by the dim lights of daily live.

Society often places an expectation on individuals to maintain a cheerful and carefree demeanour, especially in social gatherings. Peoples discomfort can often make other people uncomfortable and as a society we are taught "manners' so when asked how we are we will politely reply that we are good, often, even when we aren't, as of course we don't want to burden others. This pressure to present a happy facade can be overwhelming, leading individuals to repress and bury their true feelings beneath layers of pretence. The fear of being judged, misunderstood, or burdening others with their emotional struggles drives people to conceal their low mood, internalising their struggles leading to further emotional and mental issues.

Dancing, with its rhythmic movements and lively atmosphere, can serve as a temporary escape from the weight of one's emotions, we can also relate this to the activities we regularly engage in, which is often a way to mask our feelings, how often have you assumed someone was fine "because they were out last night?" It offers a momentary reprieve, allowing individuals to forget their troubles and immerse themselves into distractions. Behind the smiles and laughter, there can be a complex web of emotions that people conceal. It is important to acknowledge that everyone has their battles, regardless of how it may look on the outside. It is crucial to foster a culture of empathy and understanding, where individuals feel safe to express their true emotions. By acknowledging the teardrops that may exist beneath the surface, we can create a more compassionate and supportive environment for all.

# Gentle Hands

**This short passage on explores the profound impact embracing the philosophy of a gentle approach to life.**

When my son was small, I often used the soft reminder "gentle hands" this phrase was often used when he was holding a delicate animal, playing with other children or holding something fragile, that needed extra care.

How lovely would the world be if we applied this to all the human connections we encounter.

It is a simple phrase, yet it holds such profound meaning. "Gentle hands". These two words encapsulate a powerful concept that has the potential to transform the world we love in and relationships we hold. Imagine a society where every human interaction is guided by gentle hands, where empathy and compassion are the driving forces behind each connection and exchange.

In a world governed by gentle hands, we could interconnect with kind caution. Recognising the vulnerability in one another, just as we my son did when holding delicate animals in the farm. Instead of causing unintended harm or inflicting pain with our words and actions we could be more intentional with our exchanges considering the feelings of others.

How different could humanity be it be if we were to prioritise listening and communication, seek to understand rather each other rather than to judge.

Gentle hands acknowledges that everyone we meet is fighting their own battles, carrying their own burdens. Instead of adding to their struggles, we would offer solace and understanding.

How lovely indeed would the world be if we applied the principle of "gentle hands" to all our human connections and actions. It is a vision that calls upon our innate capacity for empathy and kindness.

# An Attitude of Gratitude

**The word gratitude and practicing gratitude has become a bit of a trend as of late, it is strongly promoted in the wellness world that developing a sense of deep thankfulness has benefits for mental health, and wellbeing, and practicing an attitude of gratitude could have a profound positive impact on our outlook in life and mindset. Thankfully, this is one trend I can get on board with.**

My first experience of consciously practicing gratitude was around 10 years ago personally, I was going through a very difficult time, the adversity that I faced, had a negative impact on my own mental health, I struggled to deal with the world as it was. I imagine this was the first time I experienced true emotional turmoil and seen the uglier side to humanity.

I was just beginning my practice as a therapeutic counsellor, therefore I would often hear traumatic stories, sitting with my clients in their pain, coupled with my own personal hardship and internal difficulties, as an extremely empathic person this affected my outlook on life, I found it hard to understand the world, the thought of how humans can inflict so much suffering and pain on each other was a heavy reality for me to carry, leaving me often struggling to make sense of the actions of others.

I knew I had to consciously reframe my thoughts to help shift my mindset, so I took on a personal challenge of practicing gratitude for 100 days. Each of these days, I would acknowledge something positive in that day, something I was grateful for, a person, experience or thing that made me happy. My acknowledgements varied from my sons laugh, or tiny warm fingers around my hand to something simple like my morning coffee or a sunset. Some days I had to dig a little deeper but within these 100 days never once was unable to find something to be thankful for.

About a week or so into this challenge, I became aware of an internal shift, I felt lighter, I noticed my mood changing, I noticed the world around me more and more, taking heed of the little things in life and became more mindful of the beauty that surrounded me daily. Looking back now, I became a little obsessed with the sky and the sea, and I still am. You will often find me chasing sunrises and sunsets, mesmerised and delighted by the beauty of nature. I took long walks by the sea and eventually started to sea swim, regardless of the elements could find the positive in every weather condition! I see the rain as cleansing, the sun as revitalising and the wind as reinvigorating. Life became very beautiful. I became mindfully grateful of even the smallest moment. The quote "the happiest people don't have the best of everything, they just make the best of everything" became my every day.

Whatever situation or circumstances I found myself in I always tried to make the best of it, finding joy, laughter, or pleasure wherever I could, some of my favourite memories are held in unfavourable circumstances.

Whilst practicing this newfound 'attitude of gratitude" I also took a different approach when holding space for trauma stories, learning of world disasters, and dealing with lives difficulties, again I consciously decided that rather than focus on the darkness around these situations, I would always look for light throughout, for example, in times of difficulties, look for the good, look for the helpers, acknowledge the kindness, hail the humanity and recognise the compassion, for no matter how dark things can get I promise you will always find light.

Once my challenge finished, mindfully practicing gratitude became a natural way of life, I don't write a daily gratitude list or keep a gratitude journal like many do (which is great by the way) practicing gratitude now comes as natural to me as thinking.

I give thanks every day for the life that I live, the people around me and who I am as a person. I am grateful for everything that life has threw my way, for the love, the lessons, the pain, and the pleasure. My comfortable warm home and the luxuries am blessed with. The success of my career and the clients who trust me with their stories. I am grateful for my health, both my happiness, and my hardships in life as these have led me to the path I am on and made me the person I am today. I am grateful for the opportunity to share my story and live in hope that it inspires others to consider gratitude.

# Observe - Don't Absorb

**Dedicated to the empaths.**
**A reminder I come back to time and time again has a basic premise, do not absorb the energy of others, simply observe it.**

I'm often asked how I emotionally manage the job I do, how it feels for me to sit with the suffering of others, hearing stories of pain and trauma. My answer is "I observe and don't absorb". This coping mechanism is an approach I practice in my therapeutic work and apply within my own day to day exchanges. I encourage you to do the same. When we simply observe what is going on around us, we have the skill not to hold on to, to allow each feeling and experience to come and go. To live presently. It is the ability to observe and not absorb the experience and energy of others. This superpower came from years of practice, self-protection and self-regulating my own responses. Of course, when siting in the therapeutic space I experience and feel the emotion in the room. During these times, I embrace each emotion that rises in my body, permit tears to fill my eyes and welcome the ache of my heart when I witness the pain of another's persons suffering, on such occurrences I simply regulate my breath, place my hand on my heart and fully acknowledge this response until it softly passes. I pay attention to my body sensations, inviting my client to do the same, we somatically acknowledge the experience remaining fully present with the experience. Together we coregulate. Coregulation is a collaborative effort to maintain emotional balance and regulation. Coregulation emphasises the beauty of mutual support, empathy and understanding. It supports those involved in managing emotions effectively and acknowledges the interconnection in humanity. By engaging in coregulation we reinforce the feeling of connection and safety fostering a deep connection with those around us.

As a naturally empathic person I feel everything, this is part of the human experience,

empathic individuals often find themselves experiencing more suffering in life due to their heightened sensitivity to the emotions and experiences of others. Their ability to deeply understand and connect with others can be both a gift and a burden. Empaths tend to absorb and internalise the emotions of those around them, which can be overwhelming and emotionally exhausting, however if we learn to observe our surroundings, managing these intense emotions can become a lot lighter allowing us to move through each with grace. As an empath I am highly attuned to the vibrations of others and energy in the room. An incredible strength for the work I do, great craic at a party but a complete nightmare when visiting a hospital or attending a funeral. I am sure as you are reading this you will likely relate. I say this as I usually find empaths to be the nature of those reading self-development books and always working on their own self-awareness.

Empaths can often struggle with setting boundaries, as their genuine care for others makes it difficult for them to say no or prioritise their own needs. If I could give a magic pill to most people who attend therapy it would not be the generalised anti-depressant or anxiety pill you may assume, no, it would be the pill to be a bit more selfish. Again, society has conditioned us to consider putting our own needs a "selfish act' but think about, why would we not? Consider these words that begin with self – self-worth, self-esteem, self-care, self-protection, all essential ingredients for a healthy wellbeing but very much aligning with "selfish'.

Repeatedly putting the needs of others before us can lead to feelings of being overwhelmed and sometimes feelings of being taken for granted. Additionally, empaths may feel a strong sense of responsibility to alleviate the suffering they witness in the world, leading to constant worry, stress and trying to fix everything, of course we know this is impossible, but we just can't help ourselves from trying. For empaths having such heightened sensitivity to external stimuli can also make certain environments or situations challenging to navigate. Despite these challenges, being empathic allows for deep connections and the ability to offer support to others. It is important for empathic individuals to practice self-care, set boundaries, and seek support when needed to maintain their well-being and navigate the complexities of their empathic nature.

Observing without absorbing is an essential skill that allows us to navigate the world without becoming consumed and drained by it bringing clarity and presence. When we observe, we are actively paying attention to our surroundings, feeling centred in the experience.

Absorbing refers to the process of internalising and taking in everything we see, hear, and experience. This can be extremely draining for our energy field, when we absorb without discernment, we can become overwhelmed, influenced, and lose our own sense of self.

Observing, on the other hand, involves maintaining a certain level of detachment. It allows us to be present and aware. By observing, we can better understand the world around us, make informed decisions, and maintain our own individuality while really holding space for another person.

Practicing the art of observation requires discipline and self-awareness. Regular check ins and reminders. It involves being mindful of thoughts, emotions, and reactions to external influences. By consciously choosing what we absorb, we can protect our mental and emotional and even spiritual well-being.

In a world filled with constant distractions, the ability to observe without absorbing becomes even more crucial. It allows us to filter out the noise, focus on what truly matters, and maintain our inner balance with a sense of inner wisdom and peace.

# Greif

**The last act of love. Grief is love with nowhere to be go. A reluctance to let go. Grief is the last act of love we give to those who have passed.**

Coping with the loss of someone or something you love is one of life's greatest suffering but much like we learnt at the beginning of the book, sadly, it is inevitable that at some point we will all suffer the great pain of loss. As we have identified, there are times of suffering that is just too painful for words of comfort. In this passage, and in bereavement work, my intention is not providing mere words of comfort, instead my aim is to offer solace, compassion, and healing, reach out a hand to hold for comfort when yours feel too weak and extend my heart for strength while yours breaks.

## Greif is survival

The thing about grief is we don't get over it, we survive it, we wake up each day with the only intention of surviving, until eventually we learn to live our life around the grief.

Greif is the greatest suffering in life, much as love is our greatest purpose in life.

Often, the pain of loss can feel too much. An intense feeling of sadness and overwhelming sorrow. Grief is like the ocean, enormous. Interchangeable. It comes in waves, ebbing and flowing, sometimes it is calm, gentle almost peaceful, other times it is overwhelming, strong and aggressive. These are the times it can knock of us off our feet, taking the wind from our sails. The enormously of the loss weighting down heavy.

**That heavy feeling right in the pit of the stomach. We can feel like we are sinking in it.**

Other days, it is almost manageable, life continues, we get caught up in everyday life, our pain almost fleeting. A gentle wave comes to surface when we are hit with a memory or a reminder of our loved one. We slowly learn to tread water. Working to keep our head above water. Inertia, but we get through, the day passes.

Much like the waves in the ocean, our pain is fluctuating.

Do we ever learn to live well in our grief and move on from the pain of our loss? We never move on from those we love, nor would many people wish to, however, we can move forward, we can learn to live with our loss, eventually the pain easing.

We can adapt, we can move around our grief, and we can eventually rebuild our life.

The impact of the loss may continue to permeate long after our loved one has passed but with time, strength, comfort and compassion we can work through that loss, eventually meeting acceptance, and finally meeting hope. Hope for the future.

If you are struggling with grief, it is important to take extra care of yourself, healing takes time, it takes patience. There is no timeline for grief. Grief is not one emotion; it is an experience, a process. Do not compare your grief to others, each person's experience is different. It can be a personal affair, a lonely journey. Remind yourself you are not alone. Here are some protective factors to consider. Protective Factors are positive elements or conditions that contribute to resilience. They are healthy coping mechanisms to refer to.

**Protective Factors**

Take time and care. Do not try to do everything at once set small targets that you can easily achieve. Build on that. Lean into your energy and let it guide what you can manage.

Seek and Accept Support: Talk through your feelings with friends of family. You cannot travel this path alone. You need the support and care of others. Seek professional support.

Spend time with people. Grief may be so intense that you just want to withdraw or isolate yourself; take time for yourself, yes, however, lean on those around you. Get Involved in Something. Volunteer or set a project, get involved in an activity or community group.

Implore lifestyle changes. Greif can at times feel like we are out of control. Take your control back where you can. Eat well, gentle exercise, mediation and make time for self-care. Making healthy changes will also massively improve your wellbeing at this difficult time.

Pace yourself. Grief is exhausting. It takes a lot of energy to feel so intensely so often. Allow yourself plenty of time to do everyday tasks and don't over-schedule yourself. Take your rest when you need to and offer yourself some kindness allowing yourself grace.

Check in with yourself. It is important to listen to your body asking yourself what you need that day? Each day will vary. Treat yourself well do, what it takes to manage that day. Keep the faith. Things will get better. Hold on.

If you feel you are unable to cope contact your GP, seek support from a local grief support group. See below for 24-hour Crisis & free bereavement counselling. https://www.cruse.org.uk/get-help/about-grief https://www.lifelinehelpline.

# Forgive and Forget or Forgive and Repress?

**Keeping the peace for others just costs us are own, a short passage on toxic forgiveness. What it is it and why is it so damaging for mental health?**

Toxic forgiveness is an unhealthy coping mechanism that people use to avoid conflict, pretending to be unharmed by the actions or words of other. They forgive the offence and "move on" without acknowledging the pain it has caused or holding the offender accountable for the action or words that has caused offence. The reason I find most people tend to do this to "keep the peace". From a young age we have heard such phrases, we have been encouraged to "forgive and forget, just move on it is not worth the hassle", how often have you heard such phrases when voicing your upset caused by others? The thing is we don't forget, unless our feelings are heard, we repress. Repression feelings in this instance can lead to resentment and trust me resentment is a whopper of an emotion to hold, until released, resentment builds and manifest into other unpleasant feelings. So, for me to forgive and forget is really forgiving and repressing. We must always hold space for our pain, if you don't feel you can do this with the person who caused you pain, speak to someone who has the capacity to hold that space for you, for your feelings are valid and you too are worth being held.

Personally, I feel, these statements are simply a means to avoid conflict, avoidance can be extremely damaging to self-esteem and self-worth causing a multitude of issues, such as the need to people please, agree to things we don't want to do and even live a life that does not align with our values. We live outside our authentic self. When we continue to put the needs of others before our own needs, we are silently telling ourselves, they are worth more than us, their feelings are more valid and valued than mine. It is ok that they hurt me. It is not ok. Your feelings too are valid. People pleasing is not healthy for your mental health nor your relationships. These phrases can also be detrimental to our ability to communicate in a healthy manner, therefore rather than being able to communicate assertively we form a passive, or passive aggressive communication style, all to keep the peace? Let's be clear keeping the peace of others is only starting an internal war with yourself.

The next time someone causes you upset or pain, find it within yourself to address the feeling, if you can't do that with the person address it with yourself, or talk it through with someone else. Take time to process your pain, heal, retreat if necessary. You have the right to put up a boundary or take space and time to rebuild the relationship. If you need to show up differently in the relationship that's ok too. However, during times of pain or distress the most important person that you show up for is yourself.

# A Box Full of Darkness

**"Someone I once loved gave me a box full of darkness. It took me years to realise that this too was a gift".**
**Growing and healing through adversity.**

This line comes from a poem by Mary Oliver called "The uses of Sorrow". I was first introduced to the poem whilst going through personal adversity, at the time I felt trapped in a box of darkness. At the time the poem did not resonate but only through healing and recovery did I understand the true meaning and depth of these words.

It is now one of my favourite poems and one I often share.

The box full of darkness is a metaphor for the suffering we face, sometimes this suffering is unintentionally/or intentionally due to another human, it can be the actions of those we love to cause us the most harm. It would be a fair assumption that most people have been hurt by someone they love, felt heartbreak due to a relational breakdown or suffered due to the choices/actions of others. It is during these moments of despair and uncertainty, is when we find the real strength within ourselves to rise above our circumstances. In the midst of darkness, when we are at the lowest point in life, we may not recognise the light and strength from within, but it is often in the face of adversity or during the healing process, that we discover the true capacity of our resilience, courage and determination. It is through the darker times we learn valuable lessons, discover that we are capable of withstanding extreme emotional pain, adapting to change and finding hope in even the most desperate circumstances. Dark times can be transformative, can become a catalyst for growth and transformation. Now don't get me wrong, that box is horrendous to be in, it is suffocating, isolating and not an easy box to drag ourselves out of but eventually when we find our strength, sometimes with the help of others, and eventually our determination and inner strength pulls us out.

**We can't have light without dark**

Only through dark times do we see the real beauty of light, and as we begin to see glimmers of light filter back into life, we may begin the journey of healing, which often lead us on the path of self-discovery and growth. This is not an easy journey but, on that journey, and from the depths of that darkness, we discover our own resilience and the capacity to overcome.

We learn to let go of what no longer serves us and embrace the lessons that come with each challenge. The box, once seen as a burden, becomes a symbol of liberation.

Overcoming my own trauma, I began to understand that dark times where not meant to break us, but to reshape us. Prevailing trauma became a gift that taught me so much about myself, and humanity, and only through my vulnerability did I find true strength and get to know my authentic self. This self-awareness deepened the levels of empathy I felt towards others, developed my ability to genuinely connect and understand the needs for others who may be going through their own struggles.

Through this journey of self-discovery, I learnt to appreciate the light always prevails, through dark times there is always light, usually in the form of the kindness of others. I learnt to look for the light, finding solace in the smallest moments of joy and gratitude. I set myself a task to journal and make a list of 3 things I was grateful for each day, to set a soft goal of one nice thing I would do for myself each day, and as I shared earlier record/capture a happy moment in each day, this simple daily task helped to reframe my thoughts and outlook.

So, I urge you, when you feel strong enough again, carry the lessons you too may have learnt from your own personal box of darkness, to become beacons of hope and a lighthouse for others who may be lost in their own dark times. Offer a hand to guide those who need it and share our stories of triumph over adversity.

**In the end, the dark encounters we overcome may become a part of our story, but they do not define us.**

And as we step into the light, we realise that the gift of darkness was not in the pain itself, but in the growth and healing it brought and through this process of pain, growth and healing that we discover the true essence of our being. Learn to love ourselves. Experience love. We become whole, embracing every part of ourselves. And so, the box full of darkness becomes a symbol of transformation and empowerment. It reminds us that within every challenge lies an opportunity for growth. It encourages us to keep pushing forward, knowing that even in our darkest moments, there is light waiting to be found.

**We learn to appreciate the beauty of contrast, for without darkness, we would not fully understand.**

# Authors Notes

As we come to the end of this book, I want to thank you for reading and gently remind you that the journey of personal growth is an enduring process, an interchanging dance. As we've concluded, this lifelong performance can be challenging but with a little presence, compassion, softness, and patience we can gently dance through it with grace.

I hope you carry with you the lessons this book has offered, and the insights imparted serve as a guiding light in your own personal journey of growth and transformation, inspiring you to live authentically and presently, may the teachings in this book serve as a catalyst for an open heart encouraging you to live tenderly embracing self-love and acceptance.

Sending much love and healing wishes x

**www.adcounsellingnewtownabbey.co.uk**

**www.elementswellnessni.co.uk**

# Acknowledegments

Thank you to all who encourage and support the authenticity of my work. To my beautiful clients for their trust and faith in me, allowing me the privilege of being a small part of their healing process, not only do my clients learn from me, but I them. Thanks to my tutors, supervisor, and those who continue to guide and inspire me. Thank you to my wonderful partner, family and friends for always supporting me, loving me, showing up for me, grounding me and always giving me reasons to laugh. To my son for giving me purpose.

# Declaration

Some of the passages in this book I have had previously published on local and national publications but have since and expanded on or adapted for the purpose of the book.

Names, presentations and case studies, have been modified and fictionalised for the purpose of this book.

*Available worldwide from Amazon*
*and all good bookstores*

---

www.mtp.agency

mtp.agency

@mtp_agency

Printed by Amazon Italia Logistica S.r.l.
Torrazza Piemonte (TO), Italy